Gertie's Charmed Sewing Studio

Pattern Making and Couture-Style Techniques
for Perfect Vintage Looks

GRETCHEN HIRSCH

With photographs by Shameless Photo (Angela Altus) and Meredith Heuer and illustrations by Robin Blair

ABRAMS, NEW YORK

CONTENTS

INTRODUCTION

The Charmed Studio

Making Vintage-Inspired Sewing Patterns in a Modern World

Welcome to the Charm Patterns studio! About sixty miles north of New York City, in the heart of a gilded-age Hudson River town, you may see an old industrial building tucked off Liberty Street. Go inside and you'll find a pink studio packed with petticoats, dress forms, and fabric bursting out of every nook and cranny. You may even be greeted by Elvira, our head mouser and the most glamorous studio cat ever.

Here at Charm, we make vintage-inspired patterns for the modern sewist, and we want to take you behind the scenes to show you how the magic happens. This book explores late 1940s to early 1960s fashion history using the development of several classic Charm patterns to share the design details, construction, and techniques used by vintage designers—techniques that you can still use today.

The first part of the book is devoted to a shortlist of iconic vintage-inspired designs, taking you on a journey through the historical context for the design, the pattern development process, and tips to re-create the gorgeous garments themselves. Along the way, I'll share sketches, process photos, fabric images, and a bounty of historical ephemera.

Although I am focusing on the history and birth of iconic fashion moments, it wouldn't be a Gertie book without sewing patterns! So, in Part Two, you will find three of my favorite (and hardest to find) vintage designs, re-created for the modern sewist—and I will show you how to make each one. You can find the downloadable patterns in our full size range (2-20 and 18-34, with separate A-H cup sizes) along with video tutorials and resources at Charmpatterns.com/charmedstudio-resources.

Welcome to the studio; I am looking forward to sewing with you!

XOXO,

Gertie

PART ONE

Gertie's Charmed Studio

Every day at Charm is different, but the mission is the same. Surrounded by vintage dresses and bolts of *muslin*,* we research, draft, test, fit, and test again. (And again.) Each pattern we make starts out as a mere inkling of something beautiful from decades past, and we strive to re-create it using modern technology and materials. Join me as we dive headfirst into some of my favorite garments from Charm's collection and how they became the inspiration for patterns created for today's most passionate sewists and vintage lovers.

*See Glossary on page 196 for definitions of bold italicized terms throughout this book.

ABOVE: The rack in the pattern testing area holds the key components of every project we're working on, from inspiration garments and muslins to the paper pattern pieces from every test. OPPOSITE: We often test two different sleeves on one muslin; using foundation garments and petticoats is a must for getting the fit right.

1

The Structured Shaheen Dress

As long as I've been interested in vintage clothing, I've been inspired by the work of Hawaiian designers from the fifties. In my early days of shopping and researching vintage, I was fascinated by dresses and playsuits with the labels Alfred Shaheen, Kamehameha, Surfriders, Peggy Wood, Stan Hicks, and Kahala. I'll never forget walking the floor of a vintage clothing show and coming across a stunning two-piece tropical print dress and bolero. The print had a hand-painted quality with metallic ink accents, and the shaping of the bodice was glorious: It was structured with steel boning over the princess seams, giving the bustline that unforgettable fifties shape. The back of the dress had rows of elastic *shirring* to cinch in the torso and give some flexibility to the fit. (Fun fact: While textiles can last many decades—even centuries!—with proper care and storage, elastic has a relatively short shelf life, and its replacement is an important part of vintage garment restoration.) The below-knee-length pencil skirt had a *draped* faux-wrap front with a tie, drawing the eye to the hips. The bolero jacket was cropped with a cutaway front, perfect for covering one's shoulders while still revealing the va-va-voom bodice underneath. This was a magical set. The label? Alfred Shaheen. The price? $850.

Even if I could have afforded the set, I couldn't have fit into it. It was impossibly tiny, with a 25-inch (63.5 cm) waist. (Most of the vintage clothing and patterns I came across seemed to be in that range.) But that two-piece set ignited my love for Hawaiian mid-century fashion and set me off on a design path that continues to this day. (I don't think I'll ever get sick of designing this type of dress!) It became my mission to re-create garments like that Shaheen set and to make the patterns available to home sewists like me. If I really look back on it all, I can say with certainty that dresses like that Shaheen are what made me start Charm Patterns in the first place—so it's no surprise that one of my very first designs for Charm was based on that dress. I had a vision of sewists of all shapes, sizes, and ages creating their very own Shaheen homages, in whatever fabric they liked and with whatever modifications they liked. I would give them the blueprint to create this vision, but the handwork and talent would be all theirs. But before we get to Charm, let's take a little journey through Hawaiian mid-century fashion.

If you ever have the good fortune to see a rack of fifties Hawaiian dresses together, you will probably be struck first by their gorgeous rainbow

OPPOSITE: Studio shot of the Charm Patterns Lamour Dress, a tribute to Hawaiian design houses such as Shaheen and Kamehameha.

of colors and prints. Like a collection of birds of paradise, the cotton fabrics are striking in their flamboyant patterns. This was also the era of the Aloha shirt. Increasing Hawaiian tourism meant that these men's shirts were making their way back to the mainland and beyond, setting off a craze for all things tropical. The womenswear equivalent was the tropical dress, sewn in the same fabrics as the shirts, but with a very fifties twist: cinched waists, structural bustlines, and skirts that were either tight with dramatic sarong-like drapes, or fabulously full. (Some of my favorites are full circle skirts that also incorporate pleating and gathering to make hemlines that go well beyond 360 degrees). If you peeked inside these dresses, you would see extremely structured strapless or halter bodices, complete with spiral steel boning, interior bras, and sturdy cotton linings. What makes these dresses so striking to me is the combination of humble cotton fabric and couture-level engineering.

In fact, many of the sewing skills used in the bodices are taken from European couture fashion. Look at a strapless Dior dress of the *New Look* era (1947–1950s), like the one shown at right, and you would see intricate interior *corselets*, boning, padding, and *waist stays.* As the New Look disseminated across the globe and made its way to American fashion, even sundresses and prom dresses began to incorporate many of these couture sewing skills.

I've been lucky enough to work with Linda Arthur, author of *Aloha Attire: Hawaiian Dress in the Twentieth Century*, as a consultant on several Charm projects. (When a pattern incorporates elements from another culture, we now have a practice of always researching the source material to make sure we are approaching it in the most thoughtful way possible.) What I've learned from her expertise is that "Aloha wear" is what she calls "fusion fashion," a mash-up of textiles, styles, and sewing techniques. The styles and construction had their conception in European fashion, while the textiles were Hawaiian in both their design and manufacturing.

smart mixer for cocktails

alfred Shaheen sheath
29⁹⁵

LEFT: The Shaheen Sheath featured ingenious interior elastic stays that folded the neckline into pleats.
ABOVE: Metallic yardage being printed is shown alongside the models wearing designs in the same fabric.

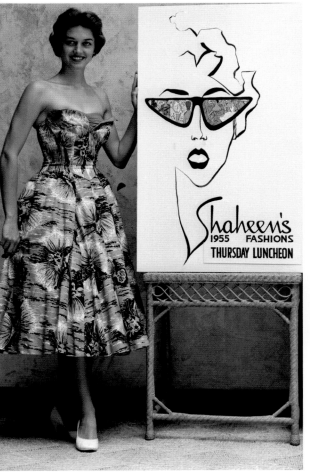

TOP LEFT: The interior of a 1950s Dior gown shows an inner corselet made of cotton bobbinet, reinforced by spiral steel boning in casings and a waist tape, with a separate hook-and-eye closure. BOTTOM LEFT: The petal bust dress remains one of the most coveted designs in the vintage world. ABOVE: This Shaheen ad boasts about the complex inner construction of a design.

Creating Structure and Shape in a Bodice

There are techniques that we can borrow from structured vintage dresses to sculpt a garment into a desired shape. I've spent a lot of time studying the support in vintage dresses (as well as reading countless books and articles on the subject), and this fact-finding mission was instrumental in shaping the techniques I use in every pattern that needs structural support.

These techniques are primarily for use in fitted bodices that must stay close to the figure and need special engineering to stay upright (rather than sagging, buckling, or slipping down as you wear them—we've all been there!). A properly made strapless bodice will stay in place through the most vigorous activity because it is anchored in place through a snug-fitting waist and supported vertically with bones and *underlining*.

Here are the major factors that go into creating this engineering:

- **FIT:** These techniques only apply to very close-fitting garments. Imagine putting boning in a caftan—what's the point? The bodice must be fitted to your body with either a small amount of *negative ease* (meaning the garment is actually smaller than your body) or only up to 1 inch (2.5 cm) of *positive ease*.

- **UNDERLINING:** Do not underestimate the power of underlining! Underlining is a secondary fabric that is basted to your *fashion fabric*, and then treated as one throughout the construction process. I experimented with different materials for underlining, from *silk organza* to fusible *interfacing*, but I quickly landed on my very favorite: humble medium-weight *muslin*. This undyed cotton fabric is usually used for making test garments in a design studio (and we certainly do plenty of that at Charm!), but it's also an economical choice for underlining. The best part is that it gives perfect structure to almost any outer fashion fabric, turning even flimsy silks and cotton lawns into bodices that will stand up on their own.

- **BONING:** This material is the star in any structured bodice. Originally made from whalebone, boning is now made from synthetic materials like plastic or polyester—but my absolute favorite type of boning is made from spiral steel. This "spiral" part means that it has two separate coils of thin steel that interlace together, like a zipper. The cut ends of spiral steel boning are very sharp, so the ends must be finished in some way. You can buy lengths of spiral steel boning cut to specific sizes and professionally finished with end caps, or buy boning yardage and finish the ends yourself (see pages 38–39). My personal preference is to buy 18-inch (46 cm) long bones with finished ends. I cut them into smaller bones as needed, and then finish the ends where I cut them. The longest bones I use are generally up to 12 inches (30.5 cm), so I can get two or more bones out of one 18-inch (46 cm) bone.

continued on next page

continued from previous page

- BONING CASING: While there are types of boning that you can sew through (rigilene is made from a polyester fiber so you can sew directly onto it), plastic and spiral steel boning require a casing. This is a tube of fabric that the bone is inserted into to hold it in place. The casing itself is what is sewn to your garment, rather than the bone. I usually sew the casing to the lining of the dress, but you can also sew it directly to the dress itself—keeping in mind that this means your casing stitching will be exposed on the outer layer of the garment. You can buy ready-made boning casing. (This is my favorite because it's very strong and also convenient if you make a lot of structured garments.) Alternatively, you can use double fold *bias* tape—or even make your own out of your dress fabric! It's worth noting that boning channels can also be created by sandwiching two layers of your garment together (say, your fashion fabric and a lining) and sewing parallel lines to make channels.

You then slip the bones into those created channels and the boning lives in the sandwich between the layers of fabric. This technique is usually used for corsets, which often have two or more fabrics layered together.

- LINING: The right lining is integral to the structure of a fitted bodice. While we often think of lining as slippery synthetic fabrics, dresses like Shaheen's used sturdy plain cotton fabrics. A cotton lining is great for a fitted bodice because it breathes, adds structure, and is substantial enough to stand up to the bones and casing you will likely be applying to it. And remember, you can always use a different lining fabric in the skirt of the same dress if you require something with a bit more slipperiness to it.

- WAIST STAY: This is an old-school trick to keep your strapless dress in place by anchoring it to your waist. *Waist stays* are usually made out of cotton petersham or *grosgrain* ribbon, finished with hooks and eyes at the back, and then tacked into your dress waistline at several key places. Another thing I like about waist stays is that they pull the boned bodice close to the smallest part of your torso, creating a cinched effect at the waist. To make a waist stay, cut a length of 1-inch (2.5 cm)–wide ribbon to the length of your waist, plus an extra 2 inches (5 cm). Turn under the ends ½ inch (1.3 cm) and press; turn under another ½ inch (1.3 cm) and press again. Edgestitch along the fold to secure. Sew hooks and eyes, positioning them so that the ends of the waist stay butt against each other when closed. Divide the waist stay into quarters, centering the hooks and eyes at the zipper opening. Mark the sides and center front with pins. Using hand stitches, tack the waist stay to the dress interior at the center front and side seams, stitching just through the lining and waistline seam allowances underneath. Fasten the waist stay to secure the dress in place when wearing.

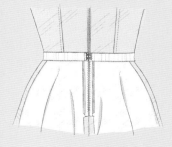

- **INNER CORSELET:** An inner *corselet* is a separate boned element that is sewn to the interior of a dress, usually one without a waistline seam to anchor bones and a waist stay to. A corselet is most often seen in very high-end garments, like vintage Dior gowns, and it's a bit like a longline strapless bustier bra that is integrated into a dress. Vintage corselets were most often made out of cotton bobbinet, a strong non-stretch tulle. The corselet is sewn with multiple layers of bobbinet, and then the entire thing is boned and often bound at the neckline in the dress fabric. A couture interior corselet is truly a thing of beauty.

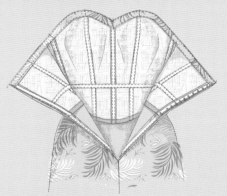

- **PADDING:** Sometimes I will use a light layer of padding or batting in designs with a cupped bust shape to give more structure and shaping to the bust. The best way to do this is to cut the bust pieces out of your padding, and then trim off the seam allowances on the bust seams. Butt the edges of the pieces together and then sew them together by machine using a zigzag stitch. You will see the shape of the cup form as you stitch. Stitch the padded cup to your outer dress cup using a ½-inch (1.3 cm) seam allowance, then trim away any excess padding from the seam allowances. Alternatively, you can use fusible batting.

First, remove all seam allowances from the fusible batting and iron it to your outer dress fabric in lieu of underlining. Sew the cups as usual. First remove all seam allowances from the fusible batting and iron it to your outer dress fabric in lieu of underlining. Sew the cups as usual.

- **FOUNDATION GARMENTS:** Even with all this inner structure, you often will want to incorporate boned foundation garments into your ensemble. Wearing a separate boned longline bra (like a vintage-style *merry widow*) will shape your body and provide the perfect canvas for your structured dress. The bra will give your body the desired silhouette, while the structural elements inside the garment will shape the dress itself and prevent any annoying buckling or slipping. If you can't find a merry widow you like in your size, you can always wear a waist cincher or underbust corset in conjunction with a regular or strapless bra.

HISTORY OF A BOMBSHELL DRESS

Early in my career in the sewing industry, I was so obsessed with the work of Alfred Shaheen that I created an online class called the Bombshell Dress, devoted to making a strong-style halter dress. In retrospect, I had very little idea what I was doing in both teaching and designing, but it still seemed to capture the attention of many sewing enthusiasts. My strongest memories of filming the class are scorching my hand with a steam iron and having to do the rest of the teaching with a bandage on my throbbing hand, and how completely in-over-my-head I felt trying to teach couture-level sewing in just a couple days while being inexperienced at both teaching and film work. What a relief that the class struck a nerve (in a good way, not in a permanently-injuring-your-hand way), and I still meet people who talk about how proud they were of their handmade bombshell dresses.

Buoyed by that success, I pitched an article on Shaheen to *Stitch* magazine, where I was a contributing editor in the early 2010s. They accepted the article concept, and I set out to learn everything I could about Shaheen. I ended up on a phone call with Camille Shaheen-Tunberg, and I was quite starstruck to learn she was his daughter. She is also the most prolific collector of Shaheen garments and knows everything there is to know about the styles and their history. Apparently, her father did not realize the historical significance of his work in his lifetime and never kept an archive of garments, so Camille took it upon herself to snatch up the designs on eBay, at vintage markets, and wherever else she could find them.

LEFT: This vintage dress is an example of how Shaheen's work shows the emphasis on the bustline, as well as his innovations with metallic ink. ABOVE: The home sewing market capitalized on the popularity of structured tropical designs. OPPOSITE: A stunning iridescent embroidered taffeta dress with a tulle shelf bust is an example of the types of dresses Mary Shaheen would have made as a seamstress.

ABOVE: Mary Shaheen was a skilled seamstress of prom dresses, adept with creating structured bodices like the ones her son designed to be made in tropical print cotton. RIGHT: Shaheen was a Lebanese immigrant to Hawaii, where he pioneered a textile industry and became known for his Hawaiian shirts and dresses. OPPOSITE: Shaheen and models in one of his textile workshops.

What I learned from Camille solidified why these dresses are so special to me—and to countless others. Her father was not a native Hawaiian, but was from a first-generation American family who emigrated from Lebanon. They settled at first in New Jersey but later relocated to Oahu. The family had a background in clothing manufacturing, and Shaheen's mother was a skilled seamstress who made prom dresses and other evening attire out of chiffon, organza, and tulle (all in the European tradition of highly boned and structured gowns). She was so adept at working with these tricky materials that when her son wanted to start a dress business using simple cottons, she was able to sew the samples like a wiz. In fact, it was Shaheen's mother, Mary, who headed up the first team of four seamstresses for the label Alfred Shaheen when it was founded in 1948. Anyone who has ever tried to sew a boned gown out of organza or chiffon will understand how telling it is that a skilled seamstress was the mastermind behind Shaheen's tropical cotton dresses.

Where Mary brought sewing talent to the label, Alfred brought entrepreneurship and ingenuity in the textile realm. At the time, there was little to no textile manufacturing in Hawaii, so fabric was imported from elsewhere, which was expensive and took months to arrive. To combat this problem, Alfred set up screen-printing workshops and devised a method for printing tropical designs directly on rayon and cotton yardage. At one point, the Shaheen workshops were printing up to 60,000 yards of fabric a month, creating a mini industry in Hawaii and providing jobs for the community. He even devised a method for printing with metallic inks along with his friend, Dr. Edmund Lutz. The inks were lightfast, and resistant to chlorine and saltwater. Printing with metallic dyes on plain cotton was quite unique at the time, and it created stunning textiles that endure to this day.

Shaheen was interested in a multicultural approach to textile design. Once his label was

established, he began sending teams of designers on international trips to gain inspiration from other cultures. These trips resulted in prints like those in his sixties Hong Kong collection, which incorporated Chinese symbols and iconography. It's worth noting that this approach was considered groundbreaking in its time, while today's consumer would likely find this to be a glaring instance of cultural appropriation. To me, this is a prime example of the need to use a critical but nuanced lens to look at vintage fashion. As we evolve in our understanding of multiculturalism, racism, and colonialism, it can be tempting to hold creators from seventy years ago to our modern standards. But I believe it's also important to look at the work through a historical framework, taking into account the designer's intent and the context of the time. (Hence, the idea of "vintage style, not vintage values" is often a rallying cry for the vintage fashion community.)

Whatever your thoughts on Shaheen's global approach to fashion, there is no denying that he is incredibly historically significant. As Linda Arthur put it best: "He was a true visionary. He started in a place (Hawaii) where there was no industry to speak of and created one from the ground up, creating a truly vertically integrated business." And along the way, he created a stunning and innovative library of dress designs that inspires to this day.

As Hawaiian tourism and interest in world cultures advanced, Aloha wear took off. The Hawaiian shirt became a staple in men's closets, and women brought home coveted Shaheen, Kamehameha, or Peggy Wood dresses and sets. The sewing industry has always kept a close eye on trends, and so in the mid-fifties through the early sixties, home sewers could re-create these looks without leaving home. Simplicity and Butterick both published patterns for Aloha-inspired designs featuring sarong skirts, structured bodices, and band collar boleros.

BEWITCHING BODICES: A GUIDE TO FIFTIES TROPICAL STYLES

Let's look a little deeper at the unifying design elements of these structured tropical dresses. Above all, the focus on these garments was on the bodice and bustline. There are several signature bodice styles in these Aloha dresses, most of them with highly engineered shapes accented with fascinating bustline details. These signature bodice designs often repeated themselves in several garments in a designer's line, with ancillary elements (skirts, shorts, boleros, straps, etc.) being swapped out to

1 Strappy ballet neckline bodice

2 Sash and drape strapless bodice

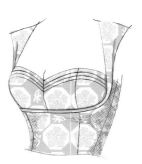

3 The shelf bust dress

4 The pleated bustline strapless bodice

5 The Shaheen sheath

6 The petal bust dress

7 The V-strap bodice

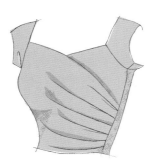

8 The Peggy Wood

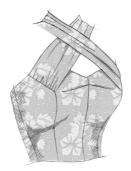

9 The Kamehameha convertible strap bodice

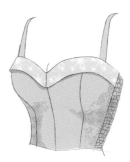

10 The neckline band bodice

create different looks. Far from being just one-off dresses, these were entire mini wardrobes consisting of rompers, overskirts, boleros, and detachable shawls and straps. I think this concept is what led me to the idea of having interchangeable patterns for Charm. Once you have a unique bodice style, it's easy to exchange the elements that go with it to create a wardrobe of amazing looks—and to challenge a sewist's creativity year after year.

Below I've detailed some of my favorite bodice styles in this genre. I've credited a specific designer where possible, but keep in mind that there was overlap between many designers, with similar garments being produced at several labels.

1. THE STRAPPY BALLET NECKLINE BODICE

A strikingly simple design, this was a *princess seam* bodice with thin straps. The neckline was scooped, with the straps emerging from the top points of the scoop. (This became known as a ballet neckline, and this style persevered through the sixties in dresses of all styles.) Kamehameha seemed to be the signature producer of this style, and it was paired with full gathered skirts for a timeless sundress. The most popular pattern I released with Butterick in my Patterns by Gertie line was a take on this bodice, and the package included both a pencil skirt and a super-full gathered skirt. I later adapted this design for Charm Patterns with additional strap options and in our full dress and cup size range.

2. SASH AND DRAPE STRAPLESS BODICE

The style that started it all for me—this is the Shaheen style I became infatuated with many years ago. At its heart, this is a fairly simple princess seam strapless bodice (sometimes with underbust cup seams), with pleats at the center front to further accentuate the bustline by contouring between the breasts. The princess seams were often somewhat bullet-shaped, just like the trend in bra shapes of the day. What really makes this dress special is the diagonal sash that starts at the neckline and ends at the waist, as well as the shoulder drape and sarong-style skirt.

3. THE SHELF BUST DRESS

The *shelf bust* is a style strongly associated with fifties prom dresses, but it made its way into Hawaiian designer dresses as well. A true shelf bust has a seam that goes either underneath or horizontally across the bustline. Above the seam, the bust was accented with ruffles, pleats, or gathers. Often, a strap would cradle the bust, creating the illusion of a bust . . . well, on a shelf. The primary designer of one of my favorite shelf bust styles is Kahala, and I was lucky enough to add one to my collection many years ago. The Kahala Hawaiian shelf bust dress was made in fabulous cotton prints, with a full pleated skirt. The bodice had bra cups, with the upper cup being beautifully pleated. A wide strap was inserted into the seam where the cups meet the bodice, gracefully extending over the shoulder to become almost little cap sleeves.

I re-created this style as the Liz Dress for Charm Patterns, and I can tell you that no other pattern design has tested my mettle like this one! I'll never forget testing every pleated cup in every cup size we offered, with discarded cups strewn all over the studio.

4. THE PLEATED BUSTLINE STRAPLESS BODICE

This is a fascinating style! The neckline has pleated upper cup sections (much like the shelf bust bodice) but there is no lower cup. Instead, the lower princess seam panels ended at the mid-bust point and wrapped around the sides of the pleated inset. In the advertisement above, you can clearly see Shaheen's clever use of shirring in his dresses: Not only was the back shirred, but there were shirred sections underneath the bust as well for an ultra-form-fitting look.

5. THE SHAHEEN SHEATH

I've been fascinated by this style ever since Camille, Shaheen's daughter, told me the story of it when I was researching the *Stitch* magazine article. This style had a fitted *midriff* and then an upper bodice portion, which tied at the shoulders in cute little knots. The neckline was square-shaped, with a little pleat in each corner. According to Camille, the pleat was formed by the clever use of elastic on each side, which attached the neckline to the waistline in a diagonal line, creating the pleat at the neckline without any stitching holding it in place. However, because elastic degrades over time, this feature has flummoxed many a contemporary vintage dress seller. Because the elastic hangs slack after wearing out, the neckline appears to be a wide, poorly fitting rounded shape. I've seen sellers either label the dresses as having cowl necks or try to salvage them by stitching the excess fabric down into gathered V-necks, with varying degrees of success. Because I've long been so taken with this style, it is included in Part Two as a pattern. (See page 167.)

6. THE PETAL BUST DRESS

In my opinion, this is one of the most striking of the Shaheen designs, and I spent years re-creating it into a Charm Pattern (see the Lana Dress). It has a two-layer bust design, the underlayer being a gathered bra cup design and the outer layer being a petal shape with bra cup seaming. The genius of the petal cup is that you can turn it down to form a wing shape, or wear it up to highlight its dramatic peaks. The dress design made use of shirring in the back and in the side front panels, and the bodice has a *basque waist* design, a lovely pointed shape that makes one think of Sleeping Beauty. The skirt is one of the most voluminous I've ever seen: a full circle that is then expanded even further with the use of gathers and *knife pleats* at the sides and a *box pleat* at center front.

7. THE V-STRAP BODICE

This is a somewhat odd design to me, but an intricate and lovely one nonetheless. It has a pleated bust and a lower midriff portion that extends up to the neckline in a sharp inverted V shape. Removable straps ended in a V at the center front, just underneath the pointed overlay. The convergence of sharply defined shapes makes this an especially interesting design.

8. THE PEGGY WOOD

Oh look, sleeves! Lest you think every design from this genre was strappy or strapless, I present to you the work of Peggy Wood. I think of this particular design as uniquely hers: a *raglan sleeve* bodice with a *surplice* overlap in the front, accented by pleating and shirred side panels. The pleats extended to the faux wrap skirt for a sarong look. I re-created a version of this stunning dress for one of my very first Butterick patterns.

9. THE KAMEHAMEHA CONVERTIBLE STRAP BODICE

This lovely dress was a simple princess seam strapless bodice with the addition of diagonal seams, into which gathered halter straps were inserted. The diagonal angle meant that the straps were perfectly poised to wrap around the sides of the bust and tie at the back of the neck in a traditional halter strap, or they could be crossed in the front for a more tropical look. (Alternatively, the straps could be tied in a bow at the bust front or even tied at the lower back to create a drape on the bodice sides.) I bought a version of this dress in a red and white tropical print made by Kamehameha, and I fell in love with how the halter straps flattered the wearer and created a beautiful hourglass shape. It made me think of the dresses Sophia Loren and Gina Lollobrigida wore to show their stunning figures to their best advantage. I was so taken by the Kamehameha dress that it became the inspiration for one of my first pattern designs as an independent designer.

10. THE NECKLINE BAND BODICE

What could be more fifties than a little band accenting your strapless or halter neckline? This detail is so iconically mid-century that it has come to be a staple in reproduction designs. I've always thought of this as a little collar for your bustline, and it can be made in contrast fabric for extra emphasis.

ABOVE LEFT: This petal bust Shaheen dress from my collection served as inspiration for a Charm Patterns design. ABOVE RIGHT: I purchased this vintage Kamehameha dress and fell in love with the convertible straps that could be worn three ways.

Bottoms and Boleros

Here's a sampling of the various bottoms that would be paired with the bodices—plus a few boleros for good measure! Think of all the different ways you could combine these elements for the most fabulous wardrobe ever.

Side-pocket
shorts

Sarong-style
skirt with tie

Sarong-style
skirt with
buckle

Wiggle skirt
with pleated pockets

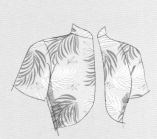

Band neck bolero

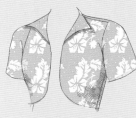

Wing collar bolero

Simple gathered skirt

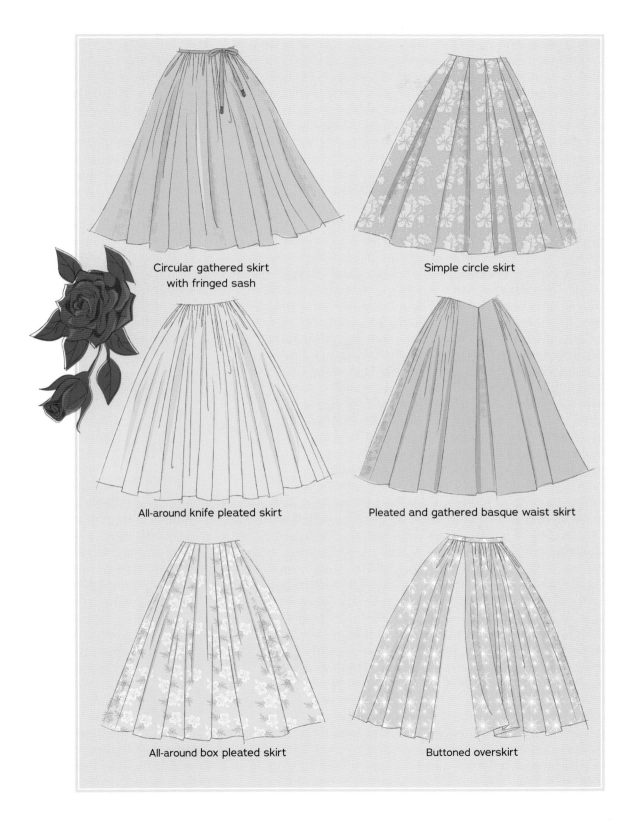

Circular gathered skirt
with fringed sash

Simple circle skirt

All-around knife pleated skirt

Pleated and gathered basque waist skirt

All-around box pleated skirt

Buttoned overskirt

A Charming Name

I named Charm Patterns after the mid-century women's magazine *Charm*. Subtitled "the magazine for women who work," it featured stunning cover photography and ahead-of-its-time headlines about income taxes, vacations, and work-life balance. Not only did I love the aesthetic, but I loved the message for modern women too (especially women who struggled to fit sewing into their hectic lives but yearned for vintage glamour). The word "charm" sums up what I love about vintage fashion: It always surprises you with its unique details and beautiful silhouettes. I also collect vintage charm bracelets, so I included a little charm icon in the Charm Patterns logo.

The Lamour Dress was named for actress Dorothy Lamour, who starred in the *Road to . . .* movies alongside Bob Hope and Bing Crosby. Though much of the humor is dated (shockingly so at times), Lamour became known for her tropical fashions in these movies, wearing draped strapless dresses in Shaheen-esque prints.

THE ROAD TO CHARM PATTERNS

In my early days designing sewing patterns (after the Bombshell Dress class, which used an existing sewing pattern), I dabbled quite a bit in structured dress styles and got a little more confident with each design. My first book, *Gertie's New Book for Better Sewing*, was an extension of the ideas explored in my first blog. One of the included patterns was a strapless bodice with ruching at the center front, and I showed how to turn it into a Shaheen-esque, faux-sarong dress using a few simple patternmaking techniques like ***slashing and spreading*** a pencil skirt to achieve the hip drape.

Emboldened, I next tried my hand at a full Shaheen fantasy for Butterick, ***draping*** a cupped bodice with the signature sash, shirred bodice panels, and faux sarong skirt, complete with hip pleats and tie. In the Butterick early days, I drafted everything and shipped them off to the Manhattan headquarters where they would be fitted on the sample-size model, crossing my fingers that the garments would fit. Later, I suggested that I model the garments myself, which made things a lot easier

when it came to fitting. (The fit model was always available!) Part of Charm's mission is to show that sewing and modeling your own garments isn't just for sample-size people—we all deserve to dress up and feel fabulous.

I designed a few more structured tropical-style patterns over the next several years, including a full beach wardrobe for Butterick that included a bustier, shorts, wrap sarong skirt, and a bolero. (Even in my early days, I had trouble restraining myself to just one idea per pattern!) And in my third sewing book, *Gertie's Ultimate Dress Book* (which included a collection of interchangeable bodice and skirt patterns), I included a basic strapless princess seam bodice and simple pencil skirt. I transformed these two pieces into a Shaheen homage in pink and gold cherry blossom brocade with the use of added elements like a hip drape and gathered shoulder strap. It was a loose interpretation of Shaheen's designs, but the real value of working on that book was that it solidified all of my current techniques.

At the time that I was writing the book and making the twenty-five (!) included sample dresses, I had just walked away from a decade-long marriage and was living in a rented bedroom and working part-time at a business that specialized in "bridal gown restoration." Let's just say it wasn't the brightest spot in my life. My responsibilities included doing the intake of gowns that were shipped directly from brides and examining them, layer by poufy layer, and creating a detailed report of all the damage the gown had incurred on the wedding day.

The dresses were shockingly expensive, and of a caliber that I'd never gotten to see up close. There were gorgeous silk twill Carolina Herrera ball gowns (with pockets!), frothy Vera Wang confections in scarlet and black, and—my least favorite—the scandalously sheer Pnina Tornai mermaid gowns encrusted in glued-on rhinestones that were all the rage in the early 2010s. While the majority of the dresses weren't vintage, the better designers often used time-tested techniques of couture sewing, so I got to examine beautifully made inner corselets, steel-boned bodices, waist

BELOW LEFT: My digital sketch showing three different versions of the Lamour Dress pattern.
BELOW RIGHT: One of the first samples of the Charm Patterns Lamour Dress.

stays, and horsehair hems up close and personal. I even saw a custom-made tribute to the Charles James Clover gown, made in ivory duchess satin and black velvet! So it was there, up to my ears in a small fortune worth of ripped and muddy wedding dresses (it was shocking how much damage could be done to a wedding dress in one day), that I ignored my own marital woes by throwing myself into studying everything I could about the construction of those wedding dresses.

DEVELOPING THE CHARM PATTERNS LAMOUR DRESS

Finally feeling that I had landed on a signature method for each step of the dressmaking process, I began to set my sights on starting my own pattern company as the next step in my career. Designing patterns for Butterick, as well as for my books, had given me the confidence to feel I could strike out on my own. I was itching to have more control over every aspect of my designs, from the sizing to the photography to the styling to the way the instructions were written.

When planning the launch of this pattern company (crowdfunded through the support of my amazing followers), I decided to start with a tribute to the Kamehameha Convertible Strap Dress (see page 17).

I'm not always lucky enough to have an original of the vintage designs I'm creating patterns based on (and not every pattern is based as literally on a vintage design as this one was), but in this case, I spent lots of time studying that dress inside and out. At its heart, the Kamehameha dress was a princess seam strapless bodice—a style that I could now design and sew in my sleep. What made this one different was the tiny horizontal pleat at the center of the bust (creating a contoured effect) and the gathered straps that were inset at an angle on the side front panel. The shape of that strap was crucially important, as was the angle it was positioned in. The patternmaking and testing process for the Lamour Dress, as I eventually

Thoughtful Tropical

When I first started in the field of pattern design, tiki designs and sensibilities were extremely popular and commonplace in the vintage community. In fact, there were (and still are) many events devoted to tiki, whether they were pool parties at rockabilly weekenders festooned with tropical drinks and fiery torches or even entire events with attendees from all over the world wearing caftans and sipping from carved tiki god tumblers. On its surface, it is a seemingly harmless tribute to (or even an ironic celebration of) a bygone era of kitsch. However, a compelling argument against tiki has become prominent within the last few years—that the celebration of tiki is really the celebration of colonialism and is harmful to Pacific Islanders. A new hashtag has emerged in its place, which I really love: the concept of "thoughtful tropical." I now use this framework when designing or styling patterns that may have formerly fallen into the area of kitsch tiki. Tropical designs are still able to be celebrated, all with the understanding that a thoughtful and considerate approach is required.

named it, was largely about getting the exact correct neckline height and shape, and perfecting the shape and angle of the straps in the entire size range. I incorporated all of my time-tested techniques into that bodice, including underlining with muslin and strategically placing lengths of spiral steel boning into casings affixed to the bodice lining. The interior was finished off with a petersham waist stay. The skirt was a simple three-quarter circle skirt (one of my favorite silhouettes), with pockets of course.

Looking back, I'm surprised at the self-restraint I showed in only having one design option in this pattern! I continue to expand the Lamour Series to this day, an interchangeable series of patterns that includes several of the bodices and bottoms shown on pages 32–33.

Using Spiral Steel Boning

Though many people are intimidated by spiral steel boning, it's pretty easy to use. You just need the correct materials and tools and you'll be making structured Shaheen-style bodices in no time. Besides spiral steel boning and boning casing (pages 21–22), you'll also need a couple of special tools.

- **WIRE CUTTERS:** Cutting spiral steel boning without the right tools can be torturous. While you can eventually manage to cut the boning with dull or weak wire nippers (the kind you may already have lying around in your garage) by gently cutting into each side of one spiral, it's much easier with a pair of heavy-duty wire cutters. My favorite is Greenlee 722, which cuts right through a bone with one pass.

- **PLUMBERS TAPE:** Also called Teflon tape, this ½-inch (1.3 cm)–wide tape can be found at your local hardware store (though I usually special order mine online in pink!). I use this to finish the cut ends of the steel bones, which can be sharp. Alternatively, you can buy metal tips for bones, but I've always found it a little tricky to get them to stay on.

Steps:

1. First, sew up your bodice lining and decide on your boning placement. My preferred placement for bones is:

   - Over the princess seams

   - Diagonally on the side front bodice

   - On the side seams

   - On the back princess seams (or back dart)

   - On the center back panel, at least 1 inch (2.5 cm) from center back

   Note: You may wish to add additional bones on the back panels in larger sizes. Some styles (like a basque waist that needs to be supported from buckling) may also benefit from a short bone at the center front that ends below the bustline.

2. Cut your casing to the length of each placement point, including seam allowances, and pin in place. For seamline placement, pin the casing directly over the seamline with the seam allowances pressed open underneath. Pin in place, centering the casing exactly over the seamline.

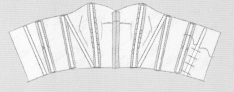

3. Stitch on each side of the casing, just next to the edge. An edgestitch foot can help keep your stitching straight.

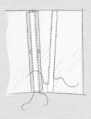

4. Sew the bodice lining to your bodice around the neckline, then *grade* and *understitch*. (Your understitching will be about ⅛ inch (3 mm) from the seamline, over your boning casings.) Press the lining to the WS of the garment, rolling the understitching to the inside for a crisp finish.

5. If the lining and bodice are now uneven at the waistline, trim the lining to match the bodice.

6. Cut spiral steel boning lengths so that they are about ⅛ inch (3 mm) shorter than the length of the boning channel from the neckline understitching to the waistline seam.

7. Wrap the cut ends of the bones with Teflon tape: Cut a 2-inch (5 cm) length of the tape and then place the cut end of the bone halfway up the width of the tape. Wrap the tape tightly around the bone, and when you are ½ inch (1.3 cm) from the end of the tape, tuck in the top of the tape and finishing wrapping. Press down on the tape to adhere it to the bone.

8. Insert the bones into the channels.

9. Staystitch the lining waistline at ⅝ inch (1.5 cm), using a zipper foot to avoid breaking a needle on the boning.

The Rita Blouse

The second pattern I published independently (also from the Kickstarter that funded the Lamour Dress pattern) was a peasant-style top called the Rita Blouse. Peasant blouses are a vintage staple, and they call to mind everything from Mediterranean glamour to Mexican embroidered pieces to Lucy stomping grapes in the famous sitcom episode. This type of top is also interesting historically, since it appears across so many cultures (Mexican, Ukrainian, Roma, Greek, and more) in so many time periods. In the fifties, we saw peasant blouses appearing on the most sultry actresses, including Marilyn Monroe in *Bus Stop*, Sophia Loren in *Madame*, and Rita Moreno in early publicity shots. It was clear that Hollywood costume designers had decided that the peasant blouse was a shorthand for sex kitten, and a kind of lush and effortless sensuality.

But what is a peasant top? Typically, it's a loose-fitting top with raglan sleeves and gathering around the neckline and armholes. It can be embellished with embroidery and is often worn tucked into full *dirndl*-style skirts. The mid-century had a special fascination with the peasant top, amping up its sexiness with fitted midriffs and often pairing it with tight pencil skirts.

The Rita Blouse (which I named for those early publicity shots of Rita Moreno) incorporated the fitted princess-seam midriff that I saw on a 1954 Simplicity pattern. This pattern has been our best seller over the years, proving the humble peasant blouse's enduring charm.

OPPOSITE: **The Charm Patterns Rita Blouse.** TOP LEFT:
Sophia Loren in a very sexy white peasant top. TOP RIGHT:
Marilyn Monroe wore a sultry lace peasant blouse in the
movie *Bus Stop*. LEFT: These home sewing patterns blend
a blousy peasant neckline with a fifties whittled midriff.
ABOVE: Rita Moreno wearing her signature look

2
The Night and Day Dress

Afterthe release of Charm's first two patterns (the Lamour Dress and the Rita Blouse), I struggled to determine my next move. I was running the business out of my house, a charming little 1930s cottage in Beacon, New York, quickly becoming overrun with vintage dresses, hats, shoes, fabric, and pattern inventory. The new business was nowhere near paying the bills, and I'd quit my part-time dress restoration gig, so I hit the ground running with two ways I knew I could stay afloat: teaching and book writing.

Over the next two years, I taught dressmaking retreats in my hometown in the Hudson Valley—and anywhere else that would have me. I traveled the world, offering two-day workshops in Australia, New Zealand, Berlin, Paris, and all over the United States: California, Arizona, Florida, Tennessee, Washington, Oregon, Maryland, anywhere! To counteract the jet lag and stress of solo traveling, I imagined myself as an international woman of mystery, jet-setting with a suitcase stuffed full of sewing notions and petticoats. It was this grand illusion that led to Charm's next pattern.

OPPOSITE: Visiting vintage shops around the globe (like the now sadly closed Faster Pussycat in Sydney, Australia) has served as endless pattern inspiration.

THE CHARM WOMAN

Besides traveling, I also watched a lot of Turner Classic Movies around this time. At this point, I worked solo and the Charm studio was the dining room, a tiny square room I'd jazzed up with chinoiserie wallpaper and a vintage Tole chandelier. The pale pink living room became my studio, and I outfitted it with a cutting table in the middle, a sewing machine tucked into a nook next to the fireplace, and a small TV. Staying motivated while working alone was always a struggle for me, so I made Turner Classic Movies my constant companion during the workdays.

I drafted patterns with Audrey Hepburn in *Sabrina* and *Roman Holiday* as my coworker and made muslins while discovering obscure older Joan Crawford movies like *The Bride Wore Red*. I paused the TV anytime an outfit took my fancy, taking notes and forming ideas for new patterns. There was so much inspiration in those old movies that I could design for several lifetimes and still not run out of ideas.

As I watched Joan Crawford in a smart polka-dot day dress with rickrack trim and a square neckline (accessorized with a chic beret), the idea for the next Charm pattern began to take shape. I wanted to design the perfect vintage dress pattern (not ambitious at all!), one that could be worn for any occasion, from a lunch date to a cocktail

ABOVE: I love anything with Barbara Stanwyck in it, so much so that I named a pattern (the Stanwyck Skirt) after her. RIGHT: Audrey Hepburn's white lace dress in *Roman Holiday* is an ongoing inspiration to me. OPPOSITE: *Gentlemen Prefer Blondes* is one of my favorite films. The smart beret and collar Marilyn wears in the movie are both so fabulous.

event. After all, many of my favorite dresses were based on similar bodice shapes, a darted **block** with a feminine neckline and **set-in sleeves**. If the Lamour Dress was my signature strapless pattern, this new pattern would be my signature darted bodice pattern.

The movies on TCM began to shape the idea for the wearers, too. The Charm woman could easily switch between gamine (think Audrey Hepburn in *Sabrina*), bombshell (Jayne Mansfield in *The Girl Can't Help It*), ingenue (Charmian Carr in *The Sound of Music)*, and femme fatale (Barbara Stanwyck in *Double Indemnity*). I had this vision of the Charm woman as a sophisticated, well-traveled vintage lover who would mix forties day dresses with smart little berets and vintage costume jewelry. I started swatching fabrics, everything from crisp striped shirting to double wool crepe to the fanciest beaded tulle. I pulled out my favorite vintage berets and perched them on my dress forms.

The seeds had been planted and the concept was beginning to grow, though it was still a little nebulous and scattered.

A DRESS FOR TEACHING

More than anything, even classic movies, teaching inspired this pattern. As I was gallivanting the world, teaching two-day dress workshops, I kept thinking how nice it would be to have one "basic" vintage-style dress pattern that all my students would use. It would be a darted bodice style so it could function almost like a **sloper**. By fitting this basic bodice together in class, my students would have a personalized pattern they could take away with them and use in a multitude of ways. And even better, the pattern would come with a variety of sleeves, skirts, and collars, so that after that first dress we made together in class (which I always required to be sleeveless and with a flared skirt, due to time constraints), they could go wild

making a whole wardrobe of dresses with that one bodice. But what would those style elements look like? I began researching dresses that were very different from the Lamour Dress: nothing that required steel boning to stay in place, but beautifully finished day dresses with the best vintage details.

In my travels, I visited every vintage shop I could. One of my favorites was Faster Pussycat in Sydney, Australia's hip Newtown area, a pink paradise filled with the most beautiful vintage dresses. (It's sadly since closed its doors for good.)

I tried on two exquisite dresses. The first was a dove grey silk shantung halter dress with the loveliest little origami-like beaded floral embellishments on one side of the bust. I couldn't zip it up, but I took many photos (with permission, of course). I've since seen that same dress in sapphire blue sold by a US vintage shop. It was more in line with Lamour than the next pattern I had in mind, so I mentally filed the

LEFT: The scarf collar on this flocked dress was so intriguing that I incorporated it into the Night and Day Dress pattern. TOP: This fifties wool jersey dress has a similar collar, utilizing a tab at the front neckline to thread the scarf collar ends through. BOTTOM: I love the sweet look of dirndl-style skirts and tops with lantern sleeves.

image away. Who knows? Maybe it will inspire a Charm pattern someday.

The second dress that struck me was a daytime frock in a pink floral taffeta with velvet-flocked accents. It had *cut-on sleeves*, a round neck, a pleated skirt, beautiful clear crystal buttons, and a matching belt. My favorite feature was the neckline: It had an unusual soft collar with tie-like ends that were inserted, crisscrossed, into a tab at the center front of the neckline, creating the illusion of a tied scarf without all the hassle and skill needed to make a perfect knot. I'd never seen

anything like it, and I was in love. Better yet, the dress fit me! I promptly paid the shopkeeper and I added that dress to my collection of vintage inspiration garments.

I visited antique shops all over Australia, in Sydney, Perth, Melbourne, and Brisbane. I collected vintage sewing patterns that spoke to me and helped me better understand the concept that was brewing in my mind. I found patterns with square necklines, full dramatic sleeves, tulip-shaped skirts, and uniquely shaped yokes. I was beginning to finalize the design elements of this new pattern.

Sewing the Perfect Dart

Sewing a perfect dart in a woven fabric is a bit of an art, and one that is somewhat old-fashioned. While dress shops used to be full of frocks in crisp cottons and silks fitted with bust and waist darts, today's stores are filled with stretch jersey dresses that don't need that kind of precision fitting. To get a streamlined look in your bodices, correctly sewing and pressing these darts is key.

1. Mark your darts carefully on the wrong side of your fabric, using a tracing wheel and tracing paper.

2. Bring the dart legs right sides together. Position one pin vertically exactly at the dart's point, and then pin along the marked lines (the dart "legs"), making sure that the lines are precisely on top of each other by checking the underside of the fabric as you pin. Stitch along marked lines from dart base to dart point. Backstitch at the beginning but not at the end, leaving a thread tail a few inches long. Tie thread tails by hand.

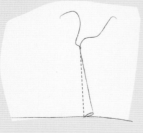

3. Lay your dart wrong side up over a *tailor's ham*, arranging the fabric so the roundness of the ham fills out the fullness created by the dart. Do not stretch the fabric over the ham, but smooth gently, making sure there are no wrinkles.

4. Press the dart toward center front or center back for waist darts and down for bust darts. Start by pressing at the base of the dart, and work your way up to the tip. The tip requires the most attention and patience. Press the tip as flat as possible, while still pressing in the correct direction.

5. If your fabric is tricky to press, you can turn the garment over and press from the right side. Just make sure to use a press cloth for any delicate fabrics and for wools, to avoid marks and shiny spots from heat.

6. Repeat steps 3–5 until the point of your dart almost disappears into the body of the garment.

THE WORLD'S MOST AMBITIOUS SEWING PATTERN

Looking back at this pattern, I sometimes wish I could go back in time and tell my younger self to cool it, that there would be plenty of time to release more sewing patterns in the future, and that I could do all the necklines and sleeves and skirts I wanted to someday. Alas, I had no one to tell me these things, and I barreled ahead with the World's Most Ambitious Sewing Pattern.

NECKLINES AND COLLARS

ROUND: I decided on a high round neckline (lower than a boatneck, higher than a scoop) that could be sewn with or without the scarf-tie collar based on that pink flocked dress I bought in Sydney.

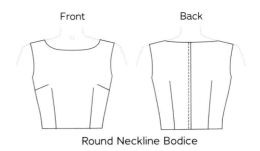

Front   Back

Round Neckline Bodice

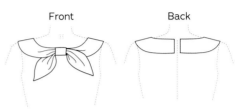

Front   Back

Scarf Collar
(compatable with Round Neckline Bodice)

Night and Day Dress

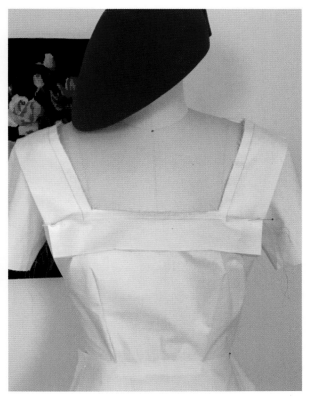

Once I'd returned home to my little dressmaking cottage, I mocked up that collar and was delighted with the result.

SQUARE: When I was traveling the world teaching my two-day dressmaking workshops, I made a dress for myself in every single workshop. I had to demonstrate on something, and I'd been given roughly 120 yards of my own fabric (designs that were being sold in the Australia and New Zealand fabric chain Spotlight). When I grew bored with the necklines in the patterns we were using in class, I began drafting new options. One of my very favorites was a square neck, a refreshing change from rounded necklines and so becoming. I knew I wanted to include a square neckline option in this pattern, and I had come across an amazing type of vintage square collar I knew I wanted to include as well.

It was a *mitered* collar, meaning that it had a diagonal seam in each corner—a fabulous way to showcase stripes that met on the *bias*. I studied vintage patterns, started drafting my version of this collar, and loved the result in *muslin*. It's just the type of thing Joan Crawford might have worn with a jaunty beret in her younger days!

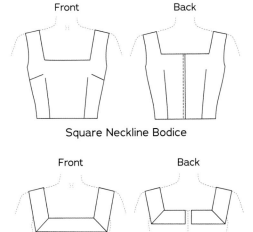

Front   Back

Square Neckline Bodice

Front   Back

Square Collar
(compatable with Square Neckline Bodice)

OPPOSITE: **The original sketch for the Night and Day Dress.** TOP LEFT: **A test muslin for the scarf collar.** TOP RIGHT: **Testing the mitered collar and experimenting with styling—here, with a beret I made in millinery class.**

SKIRTS

I knew I wanted the pattern to have at least three skirts in a nice variety of silhouettes.

FLARED: My absolute favorite skirt pattern at that time was a three-quarter circle skirt. Even though I had included one in the Lamour Dress, I couldn't imagine not adding one to this new pattern. To jazz it up a bit, I decided to add a seam down the center front and the option of cutting the skirt on the bias with stripes. This meant you could cut your fabric strategically to achieve a chevron effect at the center front and center back of the skirt, a technique that would be the perfect match for the mitered collar in stripes.

GATHERED YOKE: From my years of poring over vintage patterns, one skirt style I was especially struck by was a full skirt with a fitted yoke. This meant that the upper hips were very slim, with no gathering or pleating (imagine the top of a pencil skirt), and then there was a seam at the lower hips that attached to a very full gathered lower skirt. I loved how it kept the silhouette slim at the waist and hips while still achieving the iconic full-skirt hem of the fifties. My research showed that many patterns were drafted with a combined flat upper yoke and front panel that extended down to the hem, and then an inverted corner that gathered side panels were set into—a little awkward to sew, but worth it.

TRUMPET: For a slim skirt option, the obvious choice might have been a pencil skirt. But after years of including pencil skirts in my designs for Butterick patterns, I was a little tired of them. Though relatively easy to sew and draft, I was always plagued by the decision of whether to

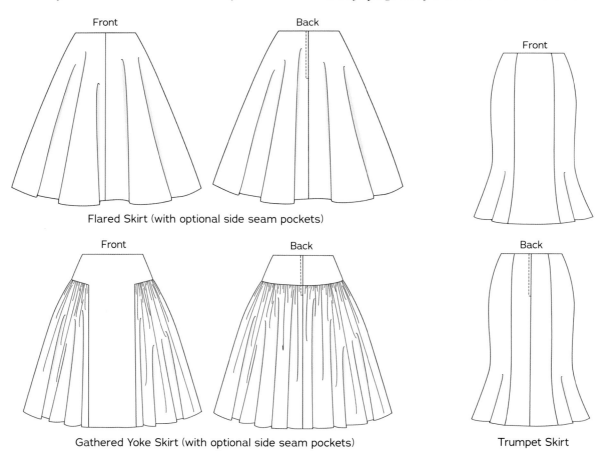

Flared Skirt (with optional side seam pockets)

Gathered Yoke Skirt (with optional side seam pockets)

Trumpet Skirt

include a simple slit (which was easy to sew but not that elegant) or a vent (trickier to sew, and nearly impossible to line, but lovely to wear and look at). I decided to do away with the whole question and try something new. I went with a thirties silhouette of a trumpet skirt, which is slim at the hip and knee, and then flares out below the knee, allowing easy walking and creating a flouncy shape. I drafted the skirt in panels (three in the front, four in the back) that flared out at the bottom. This style always makes me think of the gorgeous Ann Reinking in my favorite childhood movie, *Annie*—she was the epitome of glamour to me, and I loved the way her flared skirts moved as she danced.

SLEEVES

Sleeves can be tough for a pattern designer; it seems like everyone has a very specific preference, and it's hard to please everyone. While I personally love sleeveless dresses, there is a huge contingent of women who just won't wear them, ever. I wanted to add a nice variety of sleeves to fit any occasion. Since this bodice style has a traditional armhole, it's relatively simple to make it sleeveless and add a good sampling of set-in sleeve styles to mix and match.

SHORT WITH CUFF: This set-in sleeve has a slim profile, short length, and optional cuff with a scalloped shape. It gives a sweet-yet-polished look to a vintage style dress.

THREE-QUARTER WITH SHAPED HEM: A three-quarter sleeve is a vintage must, but I wanted to give it a little extra pizzazz. Instead of the traditional straight hem, I decided on a shaped hem with a scalloped point on the outside of the arm, finished with a facing on the inside.

ELBOW-LENGTH BISHOP SLEEVE: Now here comes the real drama! Bishop sleeves are one of my absolute favorite sleeve types: a bell-shaped sleeve gathered at the bottom and finished off with a cuff or band. They can scream femme fatale or ingenue, depending on the fabric and the length of the sleeve. I decided I wanted both vibes in one pattern! This elbow-length bishop sleeve is very "Sixteen Going on Seventeen," if you know what I mean.

LONG BISHOP SLEEVE: The femme fatale moment. This long bishop sleeve is pure forties glamour, especially in a drapey fabric. It's drafted to be "too long," extending several inches past the wrist. Then it's gathered into a slim-fitting band, which allows the excess length to pool over the wrist beautifully.

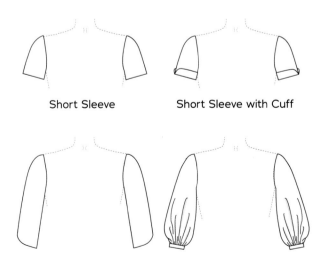

Short Sleeve

Short Sleeve with Cuff

Three-Quarter Sleeve with Shaped Hem

Elbow-Length Bishop Sleeve with Band

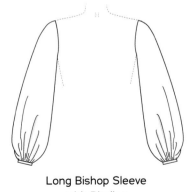

Long Bishop Sleeve with Binding

Dart Fitting

While darted bodices are considered the most basic blocks of the pattern world, I have found they can be the most challenging to fit. Here are a few of my top tips for fitting bodices with darts.

- Always make a muslin! Trust me, this is one style you're going to want to try out before diving in with your main fabric.

- When fitting a bodice with darts, always wear the foundation garments you plan to wear with the garment.

- Choose your foundation garments wisely. Vintage-style darted bodices tend to look best with bras that have a lot of projection to the cup. You don't have to wear a bullet bra, but look for bras with seamed cups that give your breasts a perky and slightly conical shape. While T-shirt bras and push-up bras have their time and place, they tend to flatten out the **apex** of the bust, creating a smooth surface that works best with knit garments rather than the very sculpted shape of a darted bodice.

- Check out the dart location in relation to your bust apex. Both the bust and waist darts should point directly toward your apex but not end directly on top of the apex. (It's worth noting that vintage dresses will often have darts that extend on top of the bust, though this has gone out of favor in modern times. The choice is up to you!)

- If you're seeing bubbling around the dart, the dart may be too big. Go down a cup size if possible.

- Learning the basics of dart manipulation (an elementary principle in flat patternmaking) is hugely helpful in making fit adjustments on patterns. One of my favorite books on the topic is *Design Your Own Dress Patterns* by Adele P. Margolis (first published in 1959). Once you understand the principles behind darts, you can move them, make them bigger or smaller, lengthen or shorten them, and even convert them into gathers or princess seams.

SEVENTY-TWO DRESSES IN ONE PATTERN

Once I had decided on the individual elements, the fun (and somewhat terrifying) part was putting all possibilities together. It was exhilarating because every single part of the whole was a building block for creating a dream wardrobe of vintage dresses, but a little shocking when I realized the monster I had created. I started sketching out possibilities for the samples I wanted to show and discovered you could make a whopping seventy-two dresses with this single pattern. While it was an astounding collection of possibilities, it created a unique set of problems.

At this point in my career, I was still doing all my pattern drafting by hand. I would either start with my favorite blocks and manipulate them on paper (also known as *flat patternmaking*),

or create them in a fabric like muslin on a dress form (called *draping*). I was versed in both of these methods through extensive research, nonstop reading and experimentation, and continuing-education classes. I would draft all of the elements by hand and then send them in by mail to a *pattern grader*, who would digitize them and then digitally grade them into the full size range. I would have the pattern drafts printed at a local copy shop, drive to pick them up, and then cut out and test the design in a variety of sizes. I would give feedback to the grader on the fit and any pattern adjustments that needed to be made, and the process would start again. It was a shockingly slow and frustratingly antiquated way of working, but I didn't yet have the resources to fix it.

Just a small portion of all the dresses in the Charm studio archive.

On top of all that, I struggled with finding the right grader for Charm, one who would be a steady collaborator. This dress pattern was such a beast that it scared off any potential graders. Or worse—they left me hanging for weeks while I waited for revisions to the pattern. I remember crying in a fabric store at this point, feeling at my lowest and completely alone taking care of an oversized, unmanageable baby of a project. I forged ahead anyway, planning the photo shoot and working on the instructions (another beast).

SHOOTING THE NIGHT AND DAY DRESS

I had started playing around with names for this pattern in my head. In my research, many of the dresses I was inspired by were considered "day dresses," so in my head I called it the Day Dress. I desperately wanted to roll with that name in tribute to Doris Day, loving the neat way the style and movie-star name played off each other. But I was bothered by the fact that Doris Day wasn't really known for this style of dress, since her heyday was really in the sixties. Even though she had worn dresses in the fit-and-flare fifties style in her younger days (see 1950's *Tea for Two*), when I think of Doris Day, I really think of her in a mod sixties look, pillow-talking with Rock Hudson. What's more, it wasn't really a day dress at this point. With all the possibilities, you could make anything from a casual cotton dress to a silk cocktail frock.

Around this time, I was working in my living room studio one day when *The Gay Divorcee* came on TCM. When the opening strains of the song "Night and Day" started up, I knew I had my name for the dress. While it's one of my favorite songs from this era (the lyric "[this] torment won't be through 'til you let me spend my life making love to you" just slays me), the mood and glamour were also captured perfectly in Ginger Rogers's floaty chiffon dress

as she was swept across the dance floor by Fred Astaire. Even better, the name Night and Day Dress truly captured the possibilities of the pattern. You could be as innocent as Doris Day or as sultry as Rita Hayworth, and you could make the dress to suit any occasion from a picnic to a formal cocktail party.

Now that the name was settled, I started planning the photo shoot. I had plans to work with Shameless, a pinup and boudoir photography studio that was quickly becoming a crucial component of the Charm dream team. I had sought out a pinup photographer for my first two Charm releases, since I knew they would be able to understand the vintage vision. Shameless ended up being the perfect collaborator, understanding every one of my visions, teaching me how to pose more effectively, and helping me create a vintage fantasy out of every photo shoot.

The final member of the dream team was Missy, a hair and makeup artist specializing in vintage looks. I met Missy when I traveled to California to visit Disneyland (I've always had a soft spot for the most magical place on earth), and to see Dita Von Teese perform. I managed to get an appointment in Missy's Los Feliz salon the day of Dita's show. I'd made an over-the-top Lamour Dress in scarlet silk satin with a dotted tulle underskirt, and I needed the perfect hair to go with it. Missy teased my hair into perfect big waves that looked absolutely stunning with my satin dress. Better yet, we formed an instant connection (it turned out she was a fellow seamstress and a fan of my patterns), and she volunteered to come to New York for my next shoot, which ended up being for my book *Gertie Sews Jiffy Dresses*. Thus began a collaboration that has lasted many years, with Missy being responsible for much of what I consider the classic Charm look.

Colorful seamless paper backdrops are always ready for the many photo shoots we do at Charm (in a custom-made pink holder, of course!).

Vintage Hair Tips

While I maintain that doing vintage hair is an art that requires professional training, I have picked up a few tips that have helped me when I need to do my own hair. Whether you're using your own hair or supplementing with wigs and hairpieces, there are many ways to achieve your vintage crowning glory.

- **Find a heatless curling method that works for you.** While the hair you see in photo shoots is done with heat tools, it's much easier (and easier on your hair) to use no-heat setting methods, and I am all about lazy vintage looks. My favorite type of curlers are pillow rollers (foam rollers with a wire through the middle and a fabric covering), which are easy to sleep on and more forgiving in terms of your technique.

- **Don't forget the setting lotion.** You don't have to fully wet your hair to set it in rollers (my hair would take days to dry!), but you should use some sort of product to get it slightly damp. Mousse works fine, or try an old-school setting lotion like Lottabody.

- **Find your best setting pattern.** I like some volume in my bangs, so I learned that using three Velcro rollers in a row, on the top of my head, gives me the best results. Then I use pillow rollers in rows around the rest of my head. For a lazy set, I've been known to use just one row of curlers around the base of my skull. (This gives me a sort of Veronica Lake soft waves look.) For more dramatic looks, I use lots of curlers all over my head. Then I wrap the whole thing in a net triangle scarf and sleep on it.

- **Brush it out.** A good hair brush is key! I use a Mason Pearson brush to smooth out the waves after removing the curlers.

- **Tease sparingly.** While a good stylist will tease your hair to high heaven for a shoot, that type of hair aggression is definitely not sustainable for every day! I gently tease my bangs if I want a little more lift there, and then smooth over the top layer with a small brush. Pin any waves in place temporarily with hair clips, and then use strong hold hair spray to finish.

- **Use hair pieces.** A lot of the best vintage looks can be achieved easily with hair pieces like clip-in bangs, drawstring ponytails, and braided headbands.

- **Use full or half wigs.** You don't have to use your own hair at all to get a vintage style! Many of our photo shoot looks incorporate full or half wigs, which you can have custom made.

- **When all else fails, wear a scarf.** People love an *I Love Lucy* moment when it comes to hair. I often get more compliments when I wrap my hair in a large silk scarf and tie it in a bow on top (leave some bangs or even curlers peeking out underneath) than when I spend an hour trying to get the perfect waves! Don't fight it; make a head scarf part of your signature style.

SIX FANTASIES IN ONE

The next step was to decide on the samples for the photo shoot: In other words, which elements would be utilized in each dress to be photographed, and what fabrics, trims, and accessories would best showcase the full range of possibilities? It was around this time that I started thinking of each sample as a fantasy, a specific vision to be brought to life. This made planning much more specific (and glamorous) than just picking a fabric I liked and calling it a day. Through lots of movie-watching and vintage photo research, I came up with six different fantasies. I was fanatical about choosing the right accessories for each of these fantasies, packing

a set of specific items in labeled baggies to be packed up for transport to Shameless's Brooklyn studio for the big shoot day. Here's how I created six different looks using one pattern and an array of accessories.

BOMBSHELL: This look was directly inspired by Jayne Mansfield in *The Girl Can't Help It* and Judy Holliday in *It Should Happen to You*. These blonde bombshells both wore slim black dresses and big platter-style hats in their respective films, and it's one of my favorite vintage sexpot looks. I chose the round neckline, long bishop sleeves, and trumpet skirt for this dress, sewn up in double wool crepe for the bodice and skirt and tulle embellished with jet beads in a diamond pattern

for the sleeves. The beaded mesh was intense to sew, since the beads had to be removed from the seam allowances by hand and then reinforced with hand stitching before sewing, but it was worth it. (Alternative technique: You can also smash beads with a hammer in just the seam allowances, then remove the broken bits before sewing. This requires good coordination with a hammer!) The finishing touches for the look were a huge vintage velvet hat I bought on Etsy, a magenta rose hair flower tucked behind one ear, black stilettos, and rhinestone earrings.

INGENUE: Inspired by Liesl in *The Sound of Music*, I decided on the elbow-length bishop sleeve, square neckline, and yoke skirt, made in a sweet

purple eyelet. I had specifically drafted the hem of the yoke skirt to be a straight (not flared) line, perfect for showing off the eyelet's scalloped edge. (This is similar to how you can use a border print along an edge; see page 135.) To play up the vintage vibes, I added my grandmother's gold watch and a locket necklace with a set-in amethyst. The finishing touches were purple suede pumps and a straw boater with "bonjour" in purple ribbon accents, made by one of my favorite milliners.

STENO POOL SWEETNESS: This version was my ultimate vintage-inspired day dress for the office— think Peggy in early seasons of *Mad Men*, fresh out of stenography school. I made the round-neck

bodice, short sleeves, and yoke skirt in a beautiful magenta wool/silk blend, then added the scarf collar and cuffs in a coordinating textured cotton (called *fil coupé*, a jacquard woven with tiny cut threads) with magenta four-leaf clover shapes. The *fil coupé* was sheer, so **I *underlined*** it with opaque white cotton, which made the background pop. Paired with a brown croc handbag and pumps, bumper bangs, and demure pearl jewelry, this look was all about daytime innocence.

SNOW BUNNY: The ice-skating fantasy! I love vintage snow bunny fashion like fur muffs, Fair Isle sweaters, short skating skirts, hoods, and ankle boots. When I found this icy-blue plaid wool suiting fabric, a vision started to come together. I

made the dress in the plaid with the round neck, three-quarter sleeve, and flared skirt, then added the scarf collar in white wool crepe. The plaid showcased the bias panels of the skirt by forming a chevron at center front. For my snow bunny accessories, I added a vintage ivory beaded beret, white beaded earrings, a faux fur muff, and ivory ankle boots that called to mind vintage ice skates.

FORTIES NAUTICAL: The square collar seemed like a great opportunity to play around with not only stripes, but a sailor-style ribbon trim. Nautical fashion was hugely popular in the thirties and forties, and I spent a lot of time studying the way trim was applied to naval uniforms and day dresses alike. Some of it was mitered, meaning that

a corner was created by folding the ribbon, but this effect was tricky to re-create. I constructed the square collar in a cherry red linen and then ended up applying narrow *grosgrain* ribbon in lines that overlapped at the corners for an authentic nautical look. I echoed the trim on the short sleeves and paired the bodice with the trumpet skirt. I considered topping the whole look off with a sailor hat, but ultimately decided that veered too far into costume-y territory (always a risk with vintage, to be honest!). I was overjoyed when I found a white forties straw hat trimmed with a red rose that mimicked the shape of a sailor cap without being too literal. Paired with red pumps and victory rolls expertly crafted by Missy, the nautical fantasy was complete.

INTERNATIONAL CHIC: I knew I had to show all the possibilities of using stripes in this pattern, and I wanted to show a look that was summery and casual. I found a beautiful red and blue striped shirting that felt silky smooth. Before buying it, I made sure to test what the chevron would look like when the stripes were mitered by folding the fabric into forty-five-degree angles and seeing how the stripes matched up. Some stripes are uneven and difficult to match, especially in a small area like the square collar. This stripe was perfect for the width of the collar, and the stripe pattern and color made me think of European destinations. Going with a summery international theme, I made this dress sleeveless and paired it with the flared skirt with chevron stripes up the center

I always start my styling process by laying out the fabric together with some possible accessories. Below are accessories for International Chic shown on next page.

front and back seams. For the styling, I went with a thirties beach vibe crossed with a travel theme. Round sunglasses, a blocked red beret, a vintage bracelet with travel charms, and a French straw market bag with red handles completed the look. Bon voyage!

CHOOSE YOUR OWN ADVENTURE

When I used to sew from commercial patterns for myself (either vintage or modern), one of the things that always bugged me was that there was only one finishing method recommended in the pattern. For instance, the pattern would be finished with facings but I chose a wool fabric that required a lining. Or, conversely, the pattern would call for a lining but I had decided to make a sheer eyelet sheath dress with a separate slip to wear underneath it, so I needed to

ABOVE: **Stripes can be used to great effect on this mitered collar.** OPPOSITE: **A look at a particularly quirky corner of the Charm styling area**

bind the edges instead. Obviously, a pattern can't anticipate every need, but I felt like there had to be a better way for a dress with so many style options. So, in the Night and Day Dress instructions, I used a method I had been developing that I called Choose Your Own Adventure, after a favorite book series from my childhood. At the end of each section, instead of just going directly to the next step, you would have a choice: If you were making a sleeveless lined dress, go to page 18. If you were making a dress with facings and sleeves, go to page 19. This tied into my educational focus with this pattern—since this was a fairly basic bodice, my hope was that the instructions would teach sewists that they always have options for how to finish a pattern.

DUMMY TEXT to fill out here. please use this character count (or more) to fill out- wear underneath it, so I needed to bind the edges instead. Obviously, a pattern can't anticipate every need, but I felt like there had to be a better way for a dress with so many style options. So, in the Night and Day Dress instructions (which were a beast to write), I used a method I had been developing that I called Choose Your Own Adventure. At the end of each section, instead of just going directly to the next step, you would have a choice: If you were making a sleeveless lined dress, go to page 18. If you were making a dress with facings and sleeves, go to page 19. This tied into my educational focus with this pattern— since this was a fairly basic bodice, my hope was that the instructions would teach sewists that they always have options for how to finish a pattern.

3

The Lilli Ann-Style Princess Coat

In my years in the vintage community, I've found a handful of iconic garments that are perennial favorites and are always guaranteed to fetch high prices on resale sites and at vintage shops and shows. A few that come to mind are tropical structured cocktail dresses by Shaheen, *draped* sheaths by Ceil Chapman, hand-painted Mexican circle skirts, and Horrockses floral stripe day dresses (extra points for the matching cropped jacket). Sewing patterns based on these designs go for hundreds of dollars on Etsy and eBay (always in an impossibly teensy size but just so stunningly beautiful that they're hard to resist). But I can't think of any vintage garment that can command the high prices and collective swooning that a genuine Lilli Ann princess coat inspires. So when I started Charm Patterns, I knew I would have to create a princess coat so that home sewists could create their very own beautifully tailored coat that would make them feel like royalty.

THE INSPIRATION

In the vintage world, "princess coat" and "Lilli Ann" have become synonymous. But a casual

observer may have a few questions: How did that connection start? Did Lilli Ann (whomever she is) invent the princess coat? And why's it called a princess coat anyway? Like a faithful vintage Nancy Drew, I had to do some sleuthing. First of all, Lilli Ann was not a person but a clothing manufacturer. The company was started by Adolph Schuman in 1933, who named it after his wife, Lillian (the ultimate romantic gesture!). In the thirties and forties, Lilli Ann focused their designs on suits and outerwear, with classic designs that had a few unique features. After World War II, Schuman traveled to Europe and began importing French couture fabrics to the United States. This investment in European fabric mills made garments created from the best tailoring fabrics accessible to American women.

Schuman's story was happening alongside an iconic French fashion movement. In 1947, Christian Dior introduced his *New Look*, a silhouette characterized by impossibly full skirts, hourglass silhouettes, and padded shoulders and hips. Schuman likely brought this inspiration back to Lilli Ann and the United States, along with many boats full of fine French tailoring fabrics. (Of course, there were other designers mimicking Dior's New Look, but perhaps Lilli Ann has endured as one of the best examples of this trend because of the company's access to similar fabrics

OPPOSITE: This design is called "Mystère" from Dior's fall 1947/1948 collection, and it perfectly showcases the New Look silhouette.

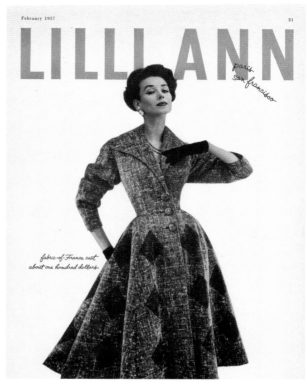

February 1957   21

LILLIANN

*paris
san francisco*

*fabric-of-France coat
about one hundred dollars*

Lilli Ann

TOP LEFT: **Famous model Dorian Leigh wears a stunning Lilli Ann suit with origami-style details.** TOP RIGHT: **This Lilli Ann princess coat features stunning velvet diamond patchwork on the skirt.** BOTTOM LEFT: **Dior's Bar Suit is the most enduring and iconic example of the New Look.** OPPOSITE LEFT: **This Lilli Ann ad has always struck me as so timeless and chic.** OPPOSITE RIGHT: **The lapels and skirt on this princess coat feature trapunto embellishment, an embroidery technique with padding that adds dimension.**

and a front-row seat in the French fashion and textile world.) After producing somewhat staid tailored garments in the forties, Lilli Ann created designs in the fifties that were wildly structural and dramatic suits and coats in imported "fabric-of-France." They hired the most glamorous models and photographers of the day, like Dorian Leigh and Richard Avedon.

Lilli Ann's coats of the fifties closely followed the lines of a Dior New Look garment: sloped shoulders, dramatic collars, fitted bodices, nipped

waists, gloriously full skirts, and tailored details
like *bound buttonholes*, *welt pockets*, *shawl collars*,
and oversized cuffs. These coats contrasted
sharply to the other popular outerwear silhouette
of the day: the swing coat, a trapeze-shaped
garment that hung loosely over a fitted frock.
Side note: I love that the fifties were all about
sharply contrasting silhouettes; it seemed you
could choose between dangerously tight wiggle
dresses or circle skirts that used yards and yards
of fabric. Coats either required a corset to wear or
hung away from the body with inches and inches
to spare.

Many of the Lilli Ann coats of this period
incorporated unique details: Some of my favorites
are velvet insets in the skirt in a series of
rectangles or diamonds, elaborate quilted panels,
trapunto stitching, and *princess seam* inserts that
converted into cocoon-like hoods—each coat
dreamier than the last!

BABY'S FIRST PRINCESS COAT

Designing the Charm Patterns Princess Coat was
a process more than a decade in the making. In
the early days of my blog, I wanted a full-skirted
coat so much that I turned the sewing process
into a painstakingly documented "sew-along,"
with videos and photos showing how I learned
the process of choosing the best fabrics, making
bound buttonholes, *pad stitching* a lapel, and
painstakingly fitting and stitching the coat. I used
a modern Vogue pattern that, to my untrained
eye, was close enough to a princess coat. (Ha!
So young, so naive.) The result was a cherry-red
wool shawl-collared coat with a black polka-dot
charmeuse lining that I still wear to this day.
That project made me fall in love with tailoring
and outerwear. I love the outdoorsy smell of the
wool as you press it, and the magical way it softly
responds to steam and coaxing with an iron. Call
me crazy, but working with the right wool can

Princess Style

Why exactly they are called princess coats is a little bit of a vintage enigma, though the answer may seem obvious to some. None of the original Lilli Ann ad copy uses this term; instead, the name appears (to me) to be something potentially bandied about only by more modern Lilli Ann enthusiasts. One theory is that many of the coats have princess seams, though that wasn't always the case. In fact, Lilli Ann made fascinating work out of darts in many of their coats, eschewing princess seams altogether. A plausible theory is that a full-skirted coat with a cinched waist is just the kind of coat a princess would wear, so the name stuck. A bit of deeper research brought me back to sewing patterns: I found some patterns from the early fifties for little girls labeled explicitly as Princess Coats and a womenswear pattern called a "princess-style coat dress." As with a lot of language, maybe the term "Princess Coat" evolved and took on different meanings throughout its life. As years have passed, I like to think we vintage enthusiasts have adopted the term for the most special, most beautiful kind of coat money can buy: the full-skirted New Look–style coat, with or without princess seams.

Butterick Princess Coat with Shawl Collar

instantly transport you to the Outer Hebrides through smell and sense alone.

When I started designing a pattern line for Butterick, one of my very first patterns was an ambitious princess coat. I took cues from my favorite vintage Lilli Ann and Dior images and made some (apparently) controversial choices: I opted for loose-fitting *cut-on sleeves* instead of *set-in sleeves* and a darted bodice as opposed to princess seams. Of course, I opted for the dramatic shawl collar and full circle skirt that is a hallmark of the princess coat.

With the Butterick pattern, I was inching closer to an authentic vision of a Lilli Ann

princess coat. (Though, to be honest, I was still so new in the field of designing that the pattern was a struggle to draft.) The real challenge of drafting this type of coat is the shawl collar, a beautiful style that defies logic when looking at the pattern. The shawl is created by continuing the lapel around to the center back of the neckline, which then creates a little inset corner on the front coat that the back neckline has to be sewn into in a slightly awkward way (see illustration on page 73, "Anatomy of a Tailored Coat"). Once you've done a few, it makes perfect sense, but it's an advanced draft for a fledgling pattern designer! As with many of my early Butterick patterns, I learned a lot from the sewing community's response. While the coat pattern was very popular, I gleaned that cut-on sleeves on a coat can be a hard sell for a modern customer, since this sleeve style always creates some *draping* around the shoulder and underarm. This draping was perfectly acceptable (even attractive) to a mid-century sewist, while modern sensibilities usually perceive this as a bad fit. (I could go on and on about how the perception of good fit is subjective and evolving, but I'll save that for another day.) Additionally, modern women tend to favor princess seams in tailored garments, as they create a much more streamlined look in tailoring fabrics and are easier to fit for many

OPPOSITE: Charm team members Andrea and Kristen review pattern pieces digitally before testing the fit.

A Sampling of Tailoring Fabrics and Supplies

Tailoring is the process of molding fabric into very structured garments like coats and suits. This structuring is achieved through the use of the correct type of fabric and supporting materials like *interfacing*. Old-school tailoring uses horsehair canvas, padstitching, and twill tape, while newer methods use fusible interfacings. Steaming and pressing is very important to the process, as steam helps the fibers retain the new shape you're training them into (like a lapel or rolled collar, for instance).

Here are some of the most commonly used materials for tailoring.

- **WOOL SUITINGS AND COATINGS:** While you can tailor fabrics like silk, linen, or cotton, nothing responds to shaping and steam quite like wool. For your first coat or suit project, look for 100 percent wool fabric.

- **HORSEHAIR CANVAS:** This is a stiff woven interfacing used in traditional tailoring. The sew-in variety must be attached to the garment with a *pad stitch*, using your fingers to shape the collar or lapel as you stitch. You can now also purchase fusible horsehair interfacing, which is applied with steam and heat and set to dry in the desired shape.

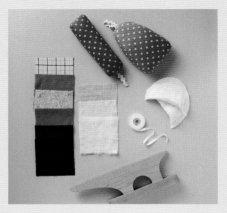

- **TWILL TAPE:** This cotton tape has a herringbone weave and is used to stabilize and shape the *roll line* of a tailored jacket or coat, creating the defined fold at the lapel.

- **WEFT INTERFACING:** This is one of the most commonly used fusible interfacings for tailoring, as it provides soft structure to woolen fabrics.

- **SHOULDER PADS:** These are essential for creating a defined silhouette.

- **LAMBSWOOL:** A lofty *underlining* which can be used to create a layer of warmth or to pad out areas of the garment, such as sleeve heads.

- **TAILOR'S HAM AND SEAM ROLL:** These pressing tools assist in shaping your garment. They're essential for all types of sewing as you build shape into your project with darts, princess seams, and regular pressing. (Note: authentic hams are stuffed with sawdust.)

- **POINT PRESSER/CLAPPER:** This dual-purpose tool has a pointed shape on the top for shaping collars and other sharply pressed areas of a garment. The base is a wooden clapper meant for beating bulky fabrics into submission as you press and steam them.

people. I took note of these modern preferences as I continued my design journey.

THE PATTERN DEVELOPMENT PROCESS

After starting Charm Patterns, I knew that I wouldn't be able to wait long before releasing a new and improved princess coat, one that would show my evolution as a designer. I had used my time between coat projects wisely, studying photos of Lilli Ann coats and even purchasing a vintage one (two sizes too small for me and wildly expensive, sigh) so that I could study the sleeves.

The sleeves! The Lilli Ann coat I purchased had my dream sleeves. At Charm, we love a statement sleeve, and these certainly fit that description. They were set-in with a lantern-like shape: fitted at the shoulder and then gracefully ballooning outward into a gentle globe shape at the wrist. I've always gravitated toward sleeves with a lantern silhouette—they are so feminine and so bold at the same time. Wearing a *lantern sleeve* says

you're not afraid to stand out from the crowd.

Though I have a flair for the dramatic (much like my sleeve patterns), I don't think I'm exaggerating when I say I was both shocked and confounded by the sleeves. Instead of achieving the lantern silhouette through seaming or gathering, the sleeve was one piece with a series of spiraling darts around the elbow. Impossibly complicated and beautiful, it reminded me of the work of Charles James, a famed couturier whose gowns were so sculptural that many could be worn only while standing up. And here was Lilli Ann, a (somewhat) humble clothing manufacturer in San Francisco, churning out coats with spiraling sleeve darts that rivaled those of James (whose garments were worn exclusively by socialites and the A-list) in terms of complexity and beauty.

I was humbled by studying that spiral-darted sleeve in the Lilli Ann coat—such a whimsical and complex detail that would have taken me countless days and muslins to perfect while creating a pattern so advanced that even the most experienced sewists might throw up their hands and choose another

pattern. And that's where the process gets really interesting for me. How can I re-create the essence of that sleeve in an accessible way?

DRAFTING THE LANTERN SLEEVE

As with lots of sewing and design challenges, there are multiple ways to reach a desired outcome. A lantern sleeve can be achieved through *slashing and spreading*, gathering, or seaming (or a combination of these). When uncertain of how I want to approach a pattern design problem, I often spend time researching vintage patterns and patternmaking textbooks and testing different methods.

I knew that gathering in a heavy wool wouldn't be feasible, so I began experimenting with seaming. A horizontal seam would be a beautiful way to achieve a true lantern shape. (Think of paper lanterns for Lunar New Year with a wide center point that narrows at the top and bottom of the lantern.) Still, the seam placement could potentially feel too clunky and obtrusive. The way to find out is to try it! I had already perfected the bodice, shawl collar, and skirt, so I had a *muslin* ready for sleeve action.

This style of seamed lantern sleeve is drafted on a one-piece set-in sleeve *block*. I started by placing a horizontal line where I wanted the seam to appear on the sleeve and cutting on the line. To create fullness at the horizontal seam (but not at the wrist or *armscye*), I made evenly spaced vertical lines on both the upper and lower sleeve pieces. I slashed through the vertical lines, leaving hinges at the armscye and wrist edges, then fanned out the sliced pieces as much as desired. (How much is desired? The trick of pattern design is that you never know until you test it in a fabric similar to the final garment fabric, so it can be a lengthy process of testing and adjusting.) The important thing is that if two pieces are going to be sewn together, they must be slashed the exact same amount, so the seamlines are the same length. And don't forget to add seam allowances anywhere you've added a new seamline.

TOP: **I own one Lilli Ann garment (which is, sadly, too short and too small for me), a classic princess coat example.** BOTTOM: **The sleeves have intricate spiral seams that create a lantern shape.** OPPOSITE TOP: **A lantern sleeve is made by first creating a horizontal seam in a sleeve block, and then slashing and spreading the fabric to give circular fullness at the seam.** OPPOSITE BOTTOM: **A warm weather, coat-dress version in floral silk zibeline.** OPPOSITE INSET: **Detail of the Charm Patterns Princess Coat**

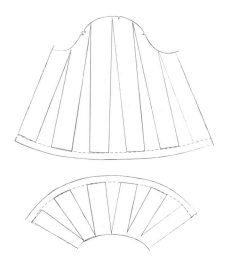

Anatomy of a Tailored Coat

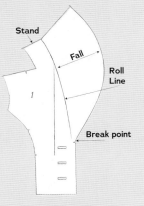

A tailored garment has several key points to be aware of as you're building shape into it. The *roll line* is the most important and should be marked on your pattern. That is the exact spot where the collar is meant to fold out to the garment, creating the lapel. (This means that the underside of the lapel is now exposed, so you see the facing rather than the coat front on the right side of the garment.) The roll line ends at the *break point*, which is where the folding out originates on the coat front. This spot is important because anything visible below the break point is the coat front, while what's visible above the break point is the facing or underside of the lapel. It's important to note the break point for fitting purposes, to guide in shaping the lapel, and so that you know where to *understitch*. You don't want any visible understitching on your lapel, so you need to leave a couple of inches free of understitching at the break point and switch from understitching on the facing below the break point to understitching on the coat front above the

break point. The *stand* is where the collar stands up around your neck, and the *fall* is what falls away to form the lapel on the shoulders and chest.

The Economics of Vintage Clothing and Modern Fast Fashion

It's fascinating to me that today we seem to have greater disparity in clothing quality between a museum-worthy designer item and something that could be bought at a high-end department store. For example, a Lilli Ann coat with all the bells and whistles could be purchased in 1956 for $100, which translates to almost $1,100 today. (Incidentally, most Lilli Ann coats have retained their value, and then some! Looking at Etsy now, I see a range from $675 at the lower end, $1,500 for one of the more coveted designs in wool, and $2,300 for a rare version in a gorgeous Barbie pink with real fox fur trim.) If you are searching for a new coat in the $1,100 range today (and let's face it, most of us aren't), you will find lovely, simple coats made in high-quality fabrics, but nothing with museum-level details.

Why this divide in cost and quality between 1956 and now? Our tastes and lifestyles have certainly changed, with most modern women favoring simple details over flamboyant ones. I would also theorize that fast fashion (the hyper-production of cheaply made trendy clothes destined for landfills and therefore creating an addictive cycle of consumption) has played a considerable role. When I started blogging, fast fashion was a big discussion topic, especially with the then recent publication of Elizabeth L. Cline's stellar book *Overdressed: The Shockingly High Cost of Cheap Fashion*. If fast fashion was shocking in the early 2000s, it's horrifying now. Sites like Shein and Cider sell cheaply made (but often admittedly stylish) coats for under forty dollars. Because I spend way too much time on Reddit, I know that younger generations have a wildly uncalibrated idea of what clothing should cost. For example, I came across a discussion of a fifty-dollar skirt, with the consensus being that the price was an outrage and the greedy manufacturer was scamming innocent consumers. For the record, I don't think this take is altogether wrong. Corporate greed, rising housing costs, wage stagnation, and inflation mean that things that were accessible to Americans in 1956 (single-income households, affordable real estate, access to education without debt) are no longer achievable. So, of course, a fifty-dollar skirt may be out of the question!

People often do not truly grasp what it takes to craft a garment until they have been personally humbled by trying to wind their first bobbin, cut silk charmeuse, or set in a sleeve. This is another reason I think sewing—and vintage pattern reproduction—is so important. Sewing doesn't always make clothing affordable (quality fabric is expensive, and my purple Lilli Ann re-creation cost $600 in supplies alone!), but with thrifting, upcycling, and bargain hunting, anything is possible.

When I tested the lantern sleeve, I knew it was the one! It wasn't an original Lilli Ann, but it captured the spirit of those vintage designs while being graceful and beautiful. Plus, it was the type of shape you never see in modern clothing, so it feels rare and unique. The only hitch was making sure the "lantern" kept its shape. Made in heavy melton wool, the form stood out beautifully and satisfyingly. But made in a thinner wool crepe, the lantern would collapse in unsightly dents. I tested a couple of different methods and found that adding a layer of fusible interfacing to the outer coat fabric gave the sleeve enough body to stand out in the intended way.

CREATING THE SAMPLES

I worked my way through the first coat sample (in beautiful, basketweave-texture purple wool), painstakingly making bound buttonholes, tailoring the collar, fully lining the coat in polka-dot silk crepe, and hemming the full gored circle skirt. As I worked, I thought about the additional samples I wanted to create for the photo shoot.

Lilli Ann was also well known for skirt suits, pairing slim pencil skirts with dramatic jackets with curvy peplums and full bell sleeves.

BOTTOM: **Original Princess Coat sketch.** OPPOSITE: **Studio shoot of the Charm Patterns Princess Coat.**

I noticed that the components of the coat (bodice, sleeves, and skirt) could easily be broken out into interchangeable elements. Further, the lantern sleeves could be broken up so that just the upper portion was used, resulting in a very Lilli Ann bell sleeve (extra fabulous when worn with opera-length leather gloves!). I also added a tailored two-piece sleeve, which could be made either full or three-quarter length. Then the skirt could be omitted, and the coat could be made waist-length (which looks adorable when paired with high-waisted skirts). And I added a peplum for a dramatic jacket look. I rounded all the options out with an additional collar look: a chic notched collar, which was just an additional stitching line on the shawl collar, but one that made a significant design difference.

I knew we had to re-create some of Lilli Ann's iconic ads for the photo shoot. Some of my favorites featured chic women in fabulous coats and walking little dogs. My Chihuahua, Hattie, is always game for a modeling gig, so she made the trek to Brooklyn with me for her Charm cover debut!

To showcase the design, I made samples in tons of different fabrics. We photographed everything, from a brown herringbone suit with a black faux–Persian lamb collar, to a bubblegum pink full-length coat with white faux-fur trim (page 75), to a floral silk zibeline coat dress for warmer climes (page 73).

Right vs. Wrong Side

Not being able to tell the difference between the right and wrong side of a piece of fabric (especially after you've cut your pattern pieces) is a common sewing conundrum. In lots of fabrics, it's easy to tell the difference, because one side will appear as a completely different color. Think of a printed quilting cotton where one side is bright and the other is completely washed out. But then there are those mystery fabrics that look the same from one side to the other. In this case, you may be able to tell by looking at the *selvage*. You may see tiny little holes on the selvage, which can be a clue. One side of the holes will be raised and bumpy, while the other is flat. The bumpy side will be the right side of the fabric. The holes are caused by little pins that hold the selvages in place when the fabric is being milled, and since the pins are inserted from the wrong side, they create little bumps when they exit on the right side. (The more you know!) In knit fabrics, you may see little glue dots in the selvage that indicate the right side.

If you've searched and studied and still can't figure out which side is the right side, you can always just pick a side. The important thing is that you stay consistent with which side you're using as the right side as you're sewing. Make sure to mark your pieces on the wrong side with chalk or an invisible-ink marking pen after you've cut them. Even if you think you'll be able to tell the difference, it's easy to get mixed up once you start sewing. There's nothing more annoying than accidentally using the wrong side of a fabric in just one panel of a dress or skirt! The mistake often becomes ultra-noticeable, in contrast to the other side of the fabric. (Even a simple twill weave will look very different in certain lights—ask me how I know!)

It's also worth mentioning that in some fabrics, like the peach-and-blue brocade used in the Rose Dressing Gown (page 82), each side may look distinct, but you're still not sure which to use. (This is especially common in brocades.) The truth is that you can use whichever side you like the most—or use both of them. Sewing a detail like a lapel or pocket in the opposite side of the fabric from the rest of the garment is a great way to make a statement.

THE HOODED RAINCOAT

After the Princess Coat's release, we got many requests for a hood addition. I loved the idea, but it was a puzzle to achieve it. The shawl collar could be extended into a large, dramatic hood—but it wouldn't be especially functional, and it would get awfully bulky when not in use. (Think of Dorothy Dandridge's hooded dress in *Carmen Jones*, designed to rest dramatically like a mantilla on the head and then drape into a cowl on the back when not in use. Gorgeous, but not meant for a bulky coating fabric!) Another option would have been a removable hood that snapped or buttoned inside the shawl collar, but I didn't love the idea of how a hood would drape over the beautifully tailored shawl collar.

So that left a third option: Draft a new coat front as an expansion. The new coat front had a simple single-breasted opening, and instead of fanning out into a shawl collar, it buttoned up to a high, round neck. The beauty of this was that it still worked with the other existing bodice pieces; it just needed a new front facing and lining pattern piece. Then we drafted a separate hood that could be sewn into the neckline. My criteria for a hood were that it was very functional and looked good both up and down. I added a tie belt, and voilà! A raincoat was born. Sewn in sapphire-blue raincoat fabric, the Hooded Princess Coat became Charm's first pattern on Patreon, a subscription-based model where we release a pattern or expansion every month.

LEFT: **Dorothy Dandridge wore this glamorous style.** RIGHT: **The hooded variation of the Charm Patterns Princess Coat, shot on my front porch.** OPPOSITE: **In the Charm studio, we order a lot of fabric swatches before making any final decisions.**

The Rose Dressing Gown

Picture it: Beacon, New York. April 2020. The whole world was deep in quarantine because of the COVID-19 virus. Charm Patterns had just launched its own Patreon, a subscription platform that delivered patterns and expansions monthly to members. I was lucky I had the success of the Patreon launch to sustain me and the business throughout the pandemic, but also entirely daunted by keeping up with a demanding new content model, all from the (somewhat claustrophobic) confines of my home.

OPPOSITE: **The Rose Dressing Gown variation on the Princess Coat (with fantasy cherry blossoms added!)** LEFT: **There was a demand for glamorous loungewear in the home sewing market, like this elegant shawl-collar dressing gown.**

One of my quarantine fantasies was a glamorous dressing gown modeled after a full-skirted yellow floral brocade worn by the character Rose Weissman in the fabulous TV show *The Marvelous Mrs. Maisel*. The timing felt magical and perfect to create something meant to be worn at home for the most elegant, and extra, kind of pandemic chic. Studying the lines of the *Maisel* dressing gown and other vintage dressing gowns, I saw a lot of similarities with our Princess Coat: a tailored bodice with a shawl lapel, slim sleeves, and a full skirt. However, my favorite examples of dressing gowns were double-breasted with just two buttons at the waist, making for a low break point and a ***roll line*** that started just above the waist seam.

I was able to design a dressing gown expansion for the Princess Coat (as for the hooded version) by replacing the center front panels to make it have a deeper overlap at center front and a lower break point. Then, knowing that the gored three-quarter circle skirt pieces would get incredibly wide when extended to floor length, I replaced them with A-line pieces without gores. (Sometimes, the width of a fabric determines the design in unexpected ways!) And speaking of fabric, it *had* to be a showstopper. I shopped at B&J Fabrics (where the *Maisel* fabric was also purchased) and landed on a peach-and-powder-blue metallic floral brocade that looks just as stunning from the wrong side as the right. This quality made it perfect for playing around with contrast on the dressing gown—I cut the lapel and pocket with the peach side facing out and the rest of the gown with the blue side out. I lined the peach silk charmeuse, and the entire effect was breathtaking. Looking back, I still think it's one of the most beautiful things I've sewn!

Of course, the photo shoot had to be done at home, which was a challenge. The cherry blossoms outside my little house were just starting to bloom, and my photo editor turned the entire thing into a truly magical quarantine fantasy by taking the existing elements and turning them into something from a fairy tale: a million swirling cherry blossoms, a wizened old tree trunk, and shimmering, otherworldly light.

I also sewed a black-and-red floral wool challis "brunch coat" version, which was knee length and lined in red silk crepe. So many looks can be achieved with one base pattern!

4

The Tropical Mermaid Gown

Let me take you on a little design journey, one that starts with a tropical-print cotton dress made in the fifties by a famed Hawaiian designer (whom we learned about in Chapter One), takes us to glamorous mid-century jazz club La Martinique, and ends in a modern-day sewing studio on the Hudson River.

THE INSPIRATION

One of my favorite vintage pieces I've bought over the years is a fifties-era Hawaiian mermaid dress by Alfred Shaheen, a designer you will remember from the first chapter of this book. Shaheen was a brilliant designer based out of Honolulu who melded Pacific prints and styles with structured fifties silhouettes, and his garments are some of the most collectible pieces in the vintage world.

On the hanger, the mermaid dress looks a bit like a standard cotton maxi dress that a woman might have bought at a resort and worn on a tropical vacation: One might even use the word "muumuu" to describe it. On the body, it has a completely different effect: The torso has both darts and princess seams to give an utterly sculpted effect. This effect is magnified especially when worn over the right foundation garments! (My favorite is a *merry widow* that is a reproduction of a fifties strapless longline bra.) The sleeves are fabulously unique: a defined lantern shape that works to enhance an hourglass shape to the figure when balanced with the dramatic box-pleated mermaid train.

THE PATTERN DEVELOPMENT PROCESS

Creating an homage to a vintage design is never exactly straightforward. My approach is to decide which features are the most important to the overall design so that I know what cannot be compromised. In the case of the Shaheen-inspired Mermaid Gown, those features were the extremely sculpted torso, the *lantern sleeve*, and the dramatic mermaid hem.

I also study the design to be aware of any pitfalls that will make the pattern difficult to sew, needlessly fussy, or impossible to re-create with home sewing methods. This particular design had a clear obstacle: the way the center front bodice panel continues seamlessly into the first *box pleat* (located at the front *princess seam*). While it looks lovely, this feature creates an inverted corner seam with a box pleat sewn into it. I could tell just by

OPPOSITE: This version of the Charm Patterns Bryant Gown is made in batik quilting cotton with a tropical floral motif, an homage to this pattern's Hawaiian roots.

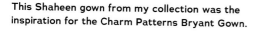
This Shaheen gown from my collection was the inspiration for the Charm Patterns Bryant Gown.

looking into it that it would induce a few choice words for our customers attempting to sew it! So I made the decision to create a horizontal seam where the box-pleated flounce could be attached without unseemly language.

This process can be useful to any home sewist! Before sewing any pattern, spend time studying the line art to really understand the construction of the piece. If there's a spot on a pattern that's giving you trouble or just seems too unnecessarily complicated, take a step back and see if you can add a seam or pare down the design in some way. Complex isn't always better,

Bryant Gown

Charm Patterns

Notes:
- front + back armhole princess seams
- lantern sleeve with elastic casing
- two fisheye darts on side front panel for extreme shaping
- flounce has box pleats at CF, CB, side seams + princess seams
- unlined, neckline + sleeve upper facings
- back capped zipper

G. Hirsch

Cotton Batik

especially when it doesn't provide enough visual payback.

As for the rest of the dress, I set to work re-creating the most crucial design details. To achieve the hourglass shape of the torso, I borrowed the brilliant use of front *princess seams* in conjunction with two *fisheye darts* on the side front and back panels. (This is definitely "extra"— to have both darts and princess seams. Usually, a dress would have one or the other, so the use of both means the designer meant business when it came to shaping the torso of this little number.)

The real challenge was re-creating the gathered lantern sleeves. Most gathered sleeves just "puff"; these had a distinct lantern shape that usually requires the use of a horizontal seam to achieve, as we learned in the Princess Coat chapter. We tried to re-create the shape in many different ways, but

TOP: Original Bryant Gown sketch. BOTTOM: I carefully dissected (and then reconstructed) the sleeve on the vintage Shaheen gown to reveal how the dramatic lantern shape was achieved.

none of them were very successful at re-creating the original intent of the dress. The first *muslin* of the dress was rather successful in all ways but one: The sleeve was a twisted, skimpy mess rather than the full lantern shape I lusted after. After many sketches, muslins, revisions, and more revisions, the sleeve continued to elude me.

In the end, I couldn't stand the agony of not knowing how the original dress was drafted, and I committed a vintage cardinal sin: I took the original dress's sleeve apart. Carefully removing each stitch and saving all pieces (for reconstruction later on, of course), I was finally able to see how the piece was originally cut.

And it was a fascinating sleeve: The deep curve on the lower edge of the sleeve (where it connects to the sleeve band) was so much more dramatic than I could have anticipated. The length of the curve meant extra gathering for a full effect, and the length at the deepest part of the curve created the *blouson* effect on the sleeve. Genius! The final part of the puzzle was complete.

Once we perfected the lantern sleeve, I decided we needed more sleeves and more ways to make the dress. Modern sewists are all about options, and I love figuring out ways to maximize a design by adding different sleeves, skirts, and collars—all interchangeable with each other so that one pattern makes many dresses. For this dress, I decided to add a short *raglan sleeve*, a three-quarter sleeve, and a cocktail-length dress option with a circular flounce.

After perfecting the pattern in muslin in the sample size, we start testing other sizes and planning the photo shoot.

DELVING INTO HISTORY

Another crucial part of the process is understanding the complete historical context for each pattern we publish, and letting that guide the styling and branding of the design. With every pattern we publish, we must be certain we are well-versed in every aspect of its history. Because a lot of American mid-century vintage borrows freely from other cultures, I have learned that it's imperative to fully understand the origin of a garment, and especially to avoid any use of sacred or religious garments, and to be sure I am not veering into cultural appropriation rather than homage. This is uniquely important with fifties designs, which were so often flamboyantly kitschy and irreverent.

I worked with a Hawaiian fashion consultant to better understand the history behind this design, and dug up my own research as well. I learned that in vintage sewing patterns, and now in the current vintage community, this type of design is often called a "holomuu," apparently a cross between a holoku (a traditional Hawaiian dress) and a muumuu. I was even able to find a similar fifties-era sewing pattern by a now-defunct company called Polynesian Patterns.

My conversations with a fashion history expert also taught me that this design is a fusion of Hawaiian fashion and European evening wear. (The mermaid-train formal gown was invented by French couturier Marcel Rochas in the 1930s.) This discovery excited me, because one of the things I love about designer Alfred Shaheen is that his garments often melded European dressmaking with Hawaiian design and textiles, a true tribute to his seamstress mother (she made prom dresses in the fifties—fabulous frothy creations with intricately boned bodices) and his Hawaiian home. This revelation led me to other mermaid-style gowns, and directly to the figure who would become the pattern's namesake.

Joyce Bryant, a fabulous Black jazz singer well known for her silver hair (she famously used radiator paint to dye it so she wouldn't be upstaged by Josephine Baker at legendary nightclub La Martinique) and curve-hugging mermaid gowns, was a welcome detour on my historical journey. I learned that her show-stopping dresses were designed by Zelda Wynn Valdes, who was known as the first Black fashion designer and who created the amazingly complex

LEFT: Joyce Bryant was famous for her platinum hair and mermaid gowns. RIGHT: Zelda Wynn Valdes, a Black designer who designed Joyce Bryant's gowns, also designed the highly corseted Playboy Bunny uniforms.

Playboy Bunny uniform. (Seriously, if you ever get the chance to look inside a bunny suit, do it! They were satin feats of engineering complete with interior corsets.)

Learning more about Bryant and Valdes, I knew that this pattern had to be partially a tribute to both of them, with the name Bryant Gown. But I also knew that the styling of the pattern would need to be varied enough to call to mind both Shaheen and Bryant: a perfect mix of vintage tropical and jazz club glamour.

CREATING THE SAMPLES

Before a photo shoot, I sketch each of the looks we are going to sew as samples and assign each to a model. This is both my favorite part and the hardest. With so many possibilities of fabrics, trims, and styling choices, it can be difficult to narrow down to a manageable amount of samples. I always feel a lot of pressure at this part too: If we can make only a handful of dresses that will tell the entire story of this design, how do I make sure the pattern is represented in the best way possible?

Often, at this point, I go back to my original source material and inspiration photos to try to reconnect with the vision for the pattern. For the Bryant Gown, that meant first going back to that vintage Shaheen dress. Of course,

The Mermaid Effect

It's undeniable that a mermaid moment was happening in the 1950s. In fact, the seeds had been planted two decades earlier with the work of Marcel Rochas, a French couturier who had been working with new silhouettes in gowns and had debuted his mermaid, or fishtail, gown in the 1930s. By the early fifties, his mermaid evening gowns had become even more dramatic: tighter hips and nipped-in knees, followed by explosions of silk and tulle ruffles cascading at the hem. (Sadly, Rochas died in 1955.)

The mermaid silhouette was soon all the rage in Hollywood, being favored by bombshells like Marilyn Monroe and Jayne Mansfield to highlight their hourglass figures.

As always, sewing patterns followed European couture and Hollywood closely, and many mermaid designs were published, for evening wear but also for short cocktail dresses and even daytime separates, taking the mermaid idea and adapting it to a wardrobe staple that every home seamstress could incorporate into her arsenal.

there had to be a tropical cotton version of the dress! I landed on a turquoise batik that was both gorgeous and economical, a twelve-dollar-a-yard quilting broadcloth that would satisfy my bargain-seeking customers. While some garment sewists are a little prejudiced against quilting cotton (and I admit I've been one of them in the past), the truth is that it can be a great choice for fifties designs with structure, like fishtail hems or circle skirts. Just don't try to use it for anything drapey, like a cowl neck!

But I needed more than just cotton broadcloth for such a spectacular gown. I wondered, "What would Zelda do? What fabric would she use to make a showstopping gown for Joyce Bryant?" I knew luxurious metallic brocades were the answer! I found some truly fabulous (and decidedly not economical choices) at B&J Fabrics, my favorite New York City shop in the Garment District.

To fully illustrate the possibilities of the dress (much like those daytime sewing patterns of the fifties), I also added a version in lavender double wool crepe, shown in cocktail length with pearls, a chignon, and nude pumps—something a modern-day lady could go for.

While shopping for fabrics, I often create digital swatch boards, images where I can visualize all the potential fabrics together to be sure that the entire color story makes sense. This is a great tool to use at home too. If you're not sure whether two fabrics work together, take screenshots or photos and create a digital collage using an app like Procreate.

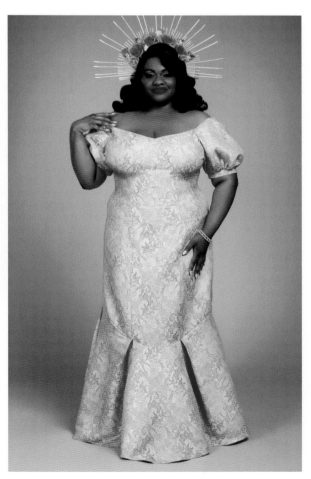

ABOVE: When planning photo shoot samples, I like to look at all the potential fabrics together to make sure they work cohesively. RIGHT: Susie looks gorgeous in a pink brocade Bryant Gown. OPPOSITE LEFT: Jayne Mansfield in a curve-hugging mermaid gown. OPPOSITE RIGHT: A Marcel Rochas design photographed by Irving Penn in 1950.

Perfect Princess Seams

Princess seams are a beautiful design feature but require a few tips for sewing them perfectly. If you look at the anatomy of a front princess seam, you should see notches that match from the center front panel to the side front panel. The side front panel will be curved outward between the notches. (The larger the cup size, the curvier it will be!) The front panel is almost always curved inward, so you have two opposing curves. (It's worth noting that on some designs, I utilize outward curves on both sides of the princess seams. This gives a very projected shape to the bustline—perfect for some fifties designs!) The side front panel seam is often longer than the center front panel seam it is being sewn to, and it must be eased in to create room at the bust. A super-common mistake made by novice sewists is to neglect to ease in the side panel, which results in excess length at the bottom of the seam.

Here are the best practices for sewing a princess seam:

1. **Staystitch the center front garment panel:** Using a ½-inch (1.3 cm) seam allowance, stitch from the top edge of the princess seam to the lower notch, then clip every ½ inch (1.3 cm) between the top edge and the notch.

2. **Sew the princess seam:** Pin the garment side front to the garment center front, matching notches, right sides together, spreading the clips so the curves match. Stitch with the clipped layer on top.

3. **For an unlined garment:** Trim seam allowances to ¼ inch (6 mm), and then finish as one. Press seam allowances toward the center front.

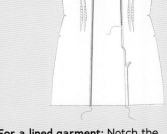

4. **For a lined garment:** Notch the side front panel seam allowances at the curviest part of the seam, cutting narrow triangles every ½ inch (1.3 cm). Press the seam allowances open.

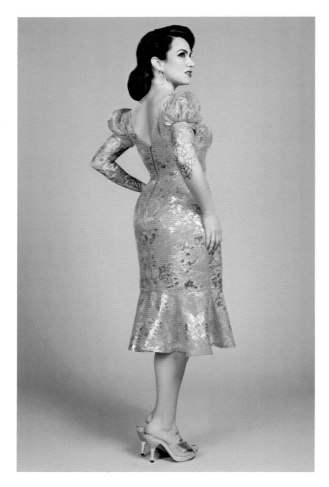

The next piece of the puzzle is styling. Charm photo shoots are all about both simplicity and vintage glamour, so I usually opt for a simple backdrop in a complementary color to the garments, and then go all out with accessories and styling. (Our motto is Feel the Fantasy, which means we're not beholden to reality when it comes to accessories!) I knew that a dramatic gown like Bryant would need to be balanced with something truly striking for headwear, so I had my lovely friend Nathaly Aguilera of La Casa de Flores create a few custom headpieces, including a blue tropical piece to be worn with the cotton batik gown and two spectacular metallic flower crowns that call to mind renaissance paintings to be paired with the metallic brocade gowns. Those looks

ABOVE: This abstract orange metallic brocade was the perfect match for this kicky short version of the Bryant Gown. OPPOSITE: We keep a rainbow of vintage-style shoes on hand for photo shoots (on a pink custom-painted rack, of course).

were the very definition of "extra," and I loved the way the accessories elevated the garments to something truly spectacular.

I encourage home sewists to take fantasy photos of their creations too. With a smartphone and a tripod, you can do so much. My biggest piece of advice is to go big for photos, because design elements always read smaller than they are in real life. Layer two petticoats, add a fake ponytail, wear those fake eyelashes, or don an enormous flower crown. Go big or go home!

MORTICIA AND BEYOND

One of my favorite design challenges is to create expansions on existing patterns: These are pieces added to a pattern that can be swapped out with the original pieces to give a different twist on the original design. And one of my favorite expansions I've done is the Morticia expansion on the Bryant Gown.

They say Halloween is like Christmas for drag queens, but I think it must be a high holiday for sewing pattern designers too. Halloween is one of the reasons I took up this career: Some of my earliest sewing memories are of my mom making our costumes at the kitchen table. I loved going to the fabric store and getting to choose the pattern for my costume, and helping pick out fabric and trims.

One of my perennial Halloween inspirations is *The Addams Family* (the 1964 television series, of course). Carolyn Jones is so sweet and sexy as Morticia, and Gomez is the perfect husband. (Despite the show's premise that they are freaks and outcasts, their loving relationship is the perfect foil to the bickering couple trope of the day.)

Looking at the lines of the Bryant Gown, I knew it could make a perfect foundation for a Morticia Gown. In fact, I was able to swap out only the train and the sleeve, replacing both with the jagged-hem shapes suitable to a dark goddess. Halloween sewing should ideally be quick and easy, so I opted to make the gown in neoprene, a spongy fabric used for scuba suits that unexpectedly was a perfect match for this project. The raw edges don't fray, so clean cuts with a rotary cutter gave the perfect batwing shapes on the sleeves and train. And instead of using facings, I applied lace flat to the neckline for a quick and easy gothic finish.

I am usually a proponent of slow sewing. Not everything has to be "quick and easy." But when sewing at home for Halloween, I make some allowances. Experiment with non-fray fabrics, skip those seam finishes, and give yourself permission to break the rules. It might just introduce you to a new technique.

LEFT: Carolyn Jones played a flawless and sweet Morticia. ABOVE LEFT: Our Morticia Gown was made in neoprene for easy, no-fray finishing. ABOVE RIGHT: Hattie serves her best Morticia in the vintage peacock chair. OPPOSITE: Batwing-shaped sleeve and train pattern pieces give the Bryant Gown pattern a spooky makeover.

The Marilyn Jeans

Jeans are such an iconic part of fashion history, but especially of the 1950s. Think James Dean in his jeans and white T-shirt, and Marilyn Monroe in cuffed form-fitting denim. Our collective image of a greaser or a fifties bad gal is not complete without jeans. I started to become interested in reproducing some mid-century dungarees after adding a couple of pairs to my growing collection of vintage clothing.

Vintage denim bears only some resemblance to modern-day jeans. The fit, construction, and fabric are markedly different. While we may think of vintage jeans as snug and sexy, in fact the fit was much looser, with a high waist, slightly dropped crotch, and wide, straight legs. Women's jeans did not have a front fly—instead there would be a zipper cleverly hidden inside the left pocket, giving a flat appearance at the pant front. As is often the case in comparing vintage with modern clothing, the fabric is wildly different. We now have the miracle (and ubiquity) of spandex in so much of our clothing, and jeans today rely heavily on spandex woven into the denim fabric to ensure a snug fit. Before spandex, jeans were made from stiff, heavy denim that took years to break in (the reason a vintage pair of jeans with just the right distressing is such a prized possession).

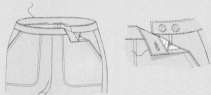

ABOVE: Susie and Hattie re-create the Blue Bell vibe. LEFT: The Marilyn Jeans have an authentically vintage hidden zipper in the left side pocket, plus two buttons to adjust the snugness of the waist. OPPOSITE LEFT: I love the contrasting jeans cuff with matching blouse in this vintage Blue Bell advertisement. OPPOSITE LEFT: Marilyn Monroe was known for her sexy looks in jeans.

In designing the Marilyn Jeans for Charm Patterns, I knew I wanted to incorporate the flat front and hidden zipper feature of vintage jeans, but also knew that I would change the fabric and silhouette for a more modern look. I slimmed the leg down and made our samples in stretch denim for comfort and a closer fit.

For the photo shoot, I took inspiration partly from a Blue Bell jeans ad, which featured a smiling mother wearing a sleeveless plaid blouse and cuffed jeans lined in the same plaid as the blouse. A timeless vintage look!

5

The Rose Marie Reid Swimsuit

The next garment on our tour of holy grail vintage items is the fifties swimsuit. While buying and studying princess coats and tropical dresses, my eye kept wandering toward these bathing beauties: *draped* sheath suits from labels like Rose Marie Reid, Catalina, Jantzen, Ceeb of Miami, and Cole of California. Some were made in the same crisp cotton as the Shaheen dresses we explored in Chapter One (more like rompers than swimsuits), while others were made of a stretchy but structured ribbed fabric. The only unifying factors were the hourglass silhouettes and the fact that they looked nothing like swimsuits of today, which are mere spandex tubes when compared with these sculptural masterpieces.

Looking at the history of swimwear in the twentieth century, there's no denying that it took a turn for the glamorous and impractical in the forties and fifties. While the early part of the century was known for wool knit bathing costumes (which just sounds absurd to our modern sensibilities), in the mid-century the right swimwear became a key part of the fashionable woman's wardrobe. No longer content to be a functional athletic piece (well, as functional

as a knitted wool cylinder could be), fabulous swimwear started gracing movies, magazines, resort collections, and celebrity vacation photos. I don't have the fashion history degree to take you through all the nuances and evolution of bathing suits of the twentieth century, but I have spent enough time studying and collecting a certain type of vintage swimwear to write with some authority on a very specific period and type of swimwear: the fifties structured sheath. As with dresses and tailored garments, I've always been drawn toward any garment that has a lot of interior structure and clever engineering, and these swimsuits are often museum-worthy examples of contouring and hidden architecture.

Imagine a strappy or strapless one-piece suit with lots of shaping: bust structure, boning, a nipped waist, and a "modesty panel": a skirted front over a full-coverage bottom. Think of Marilyn Monroe in *How to Marry a Millionaire*, and Esther Williams in every movie she ever made. This silhouette has held firm as our ideal of the retro swimsuit, and it holds so much communal nostalgia for when times were different and supposedly more wholesome.

Side note: I often get comments online from people who wish that women still dressed like this, with some twinge of longing for a more modest era. I hold none of that nostalgia myself, knowing

OPPOSITE: **This Jantzen swim sheath Marilyn Monroe wears is quintessentially fifties.**

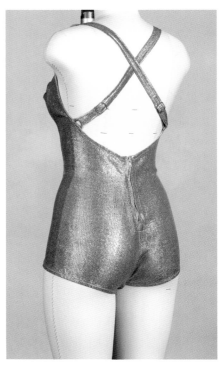

ABOVE, FROM TOP: Cotton coexisted with Lastex as a popular swimwear fabric in the fifties. This cotton swimsuit is by Alix of Miami.
OPPOSITE, CLOCKWISE FROM TOP LEFT: Shirring, structured bustlines, and "modesty panels" were emblematic of mid-century swimsuits. This fifties gold Cole of California swimsuit (from my collection) is made of Lastex. I love the colors and composition of this Rose Marie Reid Jewels of the Sea advertisement. A Rose Marie Reid suit in my collection that features bloomers, an inner bra, steel boning, and a basque waist.

that it is so wrapped up in ideals of purity and limiting choices for how women lived their lives and expressed themselves. I love these historical garments and silhouettes strictly for the beauty they possess, not for any desire to go back to "simpler times." I am happy to wear a vintage one-piece next to a woman wearing a string thong, and I am grateful that we both have the choice to dress as we please!

THE COTTON PLAYSUIT

Budding from my fascination with tropical attire (see Chapter One), I became interested in fifties beachwear, specifically rompers and playsuits. Hawaiian designers like Alfred Shaheen of course made playsuits in their signature tropical prints, but there was also a huge market for cotton beachwear from companies like Jantzen, Cole of California, Ceeb of Miami, and more. While a modern eye may interpret these pieces as casual summertime garments, they were in fact meant to be worn as swimwear/playwear at the beach and pool. Made from crisp non-stretch cotton (this was pre-spandex, after all), they often had elastic *shirring* for ease of movement. The insides were as structured as prom dresses (maybe more!), with built-in bras, steel boning, linings, metal zippers, stiff *interfacing*, and interior undergarments. And the exteriors mirrored the most elaborate cocktail dresses of the day with layered petal-like bustlines, sculptural hips, and nipped-in waists. Dior's *New Look* had an influence on swimwear, with an emphasis on creating an hourglass figure through shaping and illusion (for example, making the waist appear smaller proportionately by building up the volume of the hips and bust).

One example of this type of cotton garment from my collection is an Alix of Miami playsuit in a floral cotton accented with a grid print. It has a sweet notched bust overlay supported by boning, back shirring, and pockets that stand out from the body, creating an hourglass silhouette. Parts are reinforced with Pellon interfacing, a fusible material that has a papery, stiff feeling—just what you want when swimming! (Side note: Pellon appeared in all sorts of garments from this period. I even have an embroidered circle skirt that is entirely fused in cardboard-like Pellon, giving it a terrible feeling against the body but the most amazing silhouette when worn—it practically levitates!)

While the cotton swimsuits of this era are amazing examples of construction and design, they clearly left a lot to be desired in terms of materials. Cotton is notoriously absorbent, meaning it becomes heavy when wet. It is also easily damaged by sun and salt water. And forget trying to actually swim in these garments, because non-stretch materials hinder movement, especially when wet. (I'm not even going to get into the chafing dangers.) With women becoming more active than ever, new solutions were clearly required.

THE INTRODUCTION OF LASTEX

Fashion history often contains interesting contradictions, and one of those has to do with Lastex, a thread coated with rubber that could be woven with other materials to form a stretch fabric. Lastex was first documented in 1933, when it was used in a Sears-catalog girdle. It was used in foundation garments, a strange "beauty mask" contraption, and swimwear from the thirties on. However, cotton swimsuits still had quite a bit of popularity in the fifties, despite there being a much more advanced material available for swimwear construction. Perhaps Lastex didn't truly make its mark in a widespread commercial capacity until the mid-century, hence the continued prevalence of cotton swimwear even as Lastex was available. Or perhaps cotton swimwear appealed to the consumer who was looking more for a beach romper than for a serious athletic garment. In any case, both cotton swimwear and Lastex swimwear coexisted for an extended time in the mid-century. (They would both be overtaken

later by the invention of spandex in 1959, which is still our choice for swimwear today.)

I've had the pleasure of examining and trying on several mid-century garments made from Lastex fabric (including swimwear and a uniquely fabulous Ceeb of Miami jumpsuit—more on that later), and it truly created a miracle textile. These garments were crisp and firm, with enough stretch to comfortably mold to the body like a knit fabric.

ABOVE: This thirties ad for wool-Lastex-blend suits promised "rapid-drying" and a "smooth girdle fit." OPPOSITE: A vintage ad promotes swimsuits made from Lastex blended with all sorts of fabrics like rayon, nylon taffeta, satin, cotton, bouclé, and batiste.

Choose a swimsuit made with *Lastex* ELASTIC YARN

GUARANTEED INCORPORATING *Lastex* YARN

and enjoy perfect fit and figure control both in and out of the water

GUARANTEED INCORPORATING *Lastex* YARN

GUARANTEED INCORPORATING *Lastex* YARN

...TER PAN 606
...r suit in jacquard spun ... elasticated with "Lastex". ... Trimmed nylon taffeta and ... ribbon. Navy, Red and ... One size, fits 32" to 36" ... ...g approximately 26/6.

2 DU CROS 605 MAIDENFAIR
In Alaskan Satin woven with "Lastex" yarn. Pleats at hip and bra accentuate the deep moulded waistline. Boned inner bra; detachable straps. Powder Blue, Ice Green, Royal and Bordeaux. Selling at about £5.2.6.

3 MARATHON
"Lastex" knit trunks in a highly extensible fabric. Two sizes for boys 5 to 16 years; two sizes for men from 34" to 44" waist. Navy, Maroon, Grey, Lovat and White. From 6/6 for boys; from 9/11 for men.

4 DU CROS 601 WITCHING HOUR
In a delightful bouclé overcheck woven with "Lastex" yarn and untarnishable gold "Lurex". Interchangeable straps, and boned inner bra in Black, Powder Blue and Moss Green. Retailing approx. 4½ gns.

5 AQUALINE 638
Skirted Playsuit in a lovely "Lastex" yarn batiste. Braided trimming in self-white. Boned bra and side-seams. Adjustable halter. Black, Cherry Red, Kingfisher, in 32" to 38". Retailing about 5½ gns.

6 VENUSTAS 603
In a fine crammed check weave incorporating "Lastex" yarn. Boned bra finished with a double cuff of white and self colour. Maize, Opaline Green, Peacock Blue, Lipstick Red, Chartreuse, Black and White; 32" to 42", about 58/-.

7 MARTIN WHITE B.36
In spot print cotton, semi-skirted one piece; sculptured bra, adjusting neck strap. Elasticity and figure control by "Lastex" yarn. In Turquoise, Navy, Wine, all with white spots. 32" to 36" bust at approx. 26/-.

...REND 505
...e knitted fabric of "Lastex" ...and rayon printed with a gay ... Lifebuoy design on Black, ...isher Blue, Viridian Green, ...y, and Sky Blue. 32" to 38" ...

9 SLIX E.22
Inexpensive cotton suit in a colourful Egyptian print shirred with "Lastex" yarn for perfect fit. The well cut bra is boned and cuffed. In Red, Green, Blue, Turquoise. ...

10 SUREFIT
Self-supporting Suntop in a figure fitting fabric made with "Lastex" yarn. "3-way" halter style. In a range of smart jewel colours, delightfully printed. Retailing ...

11 JANET DICKINSON 1651
A new and most charming Rosebud print in a "Lastex" and rayon batiste. This suit possesses a very ingenious adjustable bra. Red, Gold, Royal and Mauve rosebuds ...

12 JANET DICKINSON 1609
Bloomer suit with "Lastex" yarn in a gay cotton print of Rose, Lime and Gold on Black with gay contrast. Approximately 38/11. ...

13 TRULO 935
Cleverly styled suit in a good quality rayon batiste woven with "Lastex" yarn. Has an adjustable scarf halter which can be worn four ways. In most colours. In sizes 32" to 40". From about 79/6 ...

14 CAPSTAN
Specially designed for the young teenager in a cleverly knit fabric of "Lastex" yarn and mercerised cotton. Gay polka dot design on a white ground, retailing at approx. ...

Even better, the material was appropriate for swimming, non-absorbent, and lightweight. In the fifties, swimwear manufacturers began to advertise the miracle of Lastex, linking it to figure control and hourglass shaping in glamorous designs.

THE HOURGLASS MAILLOT AND THE NEW LOOK

One of my favorite swimwear designers of the time was Rose Marie Reid, known for her movie-star swimwear. Her shapely designs are the epitome of the New Look influence and were worn by starlets like Marilyn Monroe, Jane Russell, and Rita Hayworth. Reid created lines with fanciful names like Hourglass Maillot, Sculptured Swimsuits, Draped Sheath, and (my personal favorite) Jewels of the Sea. Rose Marie ads read like poetry and elevated swimwear to high art through photography composition and color.

> *Rose Marie Reid Jewels of the Sea*
> *shape you like an hourglass, sculpt you like*
>   *a princess, send you*
> *out to swim in pearls! It's fashion, fabulous*
>   *and fanciful*
> *but always figurative . . . to add and subtract*
>   *where you need it.*
> *As witness: the duo silhouettes . . . one to hug*
>   *and one to hide,*
> *and the Fan Flare duo-bra . . . one for fit and*
>   *the other for pure flattery!*

As this ad copy suggests, much of the shaping work was achieved through creating or subtracting fullness in key areas of the body (again, much like Dior's padded shoulders and hips in contrast to corseted waists). Layered bustlines (similar to the petal and *shelf busts* we explored in Chapter One) created fullness on top, while pleated bloomers created shapely hips. The waist was made to appear smaller by contrast, and shaped slightly with boning and shirring, which held the garment tight to the figure. Rose Marie Reid once said of her designs, "A woman looks and feels her best when she is wearing an evening dress . . . I wanted that same feeling in a bathing suit."

Despite the incredibly body-conscious nature of her work, Rose Marie Reid was a devout Mormon who opposed showing too much skin. In fact, she eventually left the business in 1963 over a dispute with her partners and investors, who demanded she design bikinis to satisfy the growing demand in the market. Refusing, she said, "I don't like bikinis, and I don't want to design for a company that makes them." While the business continued under her name, Rose Marie Reid herself was no longer associated with it in any way.

Rose Marie Reid suits are my favorites to collect. The green one on page 110 is one of my personal favorites in my collection, with its beautiful scalloped overlap detail with buttons

and a crossover band at the neckline. Made in avocado green Lastex, it's fitted snugly with a high back and zipper. This suit must have been somewhat significant design-wise, because there are photos of both Marilyn Monroe and Jane Russell wearing it, and it was featured in an ad and a publicity shot of Rose Marie Reid fitting it on a model (page 109).

DEVELOPING THE CHARM PATTERNS ESTHER SWIMSUIT

After years of collecting swimsuits from Rose Marie Reid, Cole of California, Alix of Miami, and others, I became transfixed with the notion of re-creating one of these wonders in a modern way. This is probably the biggest design challenge

ABOVE: The "petal pockets" of this swimsuit accentuate the hips to create an hourglass figure. OPPOSITE LEFT: The bustline pleats of this swimsuit are reminiscent of the Alfred Shaheen dresses in Chapter One.

I've ever given myself, as the list of obstacles was never-ending. While modern women are magnetically drawn to the Dior-esque silhouette of fifties swim sheaths, almost everything about the construction is unappealing to today's sensibilities. Metal zippers, multiple bust layers, scratchy Pellon, pointy boned bust cups, and tiny snaps and hooks were all part and parcel of the hourglass maillot. But the biggest obstacle of all was sourcing a similar fabric to Lastex. The sad truth is that there is nothing similar to Lastex on today's swimwear fabric market. (If I could take a trip in a time machine, I would go back to the fifties and bring back a healthy stock of this wonder fabric, in all its various textures and colors: metallic golds, ribbed solids, pastel satins.)

When I started to consider designing a swimsuit for Charm, I knew fabric would be the main challenge. I spent a lot of time and resources ordering swatches, hoping that maybe there was something out there that would re-create the look and feel of Lastex. Stretch bengaline, "super spandex," scuba knit, stretch wovens—I explored them all! This path can be frustrating, not only because it feels like a wild fabric goose hunt. If a recommended fabric is too obscure or available only from specialty sources, the typical home sewist is unlikely to want to bother with the pattern. I started to really question the end goal for this pattern: Was it to re-create a vintage look in modern fabrics? Or to get as close to the original vintage design as possible, even if that meant using some unconventional techniques and materials? In the end, the decision was really made for me because there were just too many obstacles in the way of re-creating a vintage swimsuit as it would have truly been made in its time.

I began to explore layering fabrics to achieve the control and structure that a vintage suit would have had. Modern swimsuits are made of high-stretch spandex knits, which offer very little structure but lots of comfort, movement, and practicality. Plus they are widely available and come in a huge variety of colors and prints, a plus for the modern sewing

TOP LEFT: Rose Marie Reid designed this swimsuit for a fundraiser; it was later featured in a Lady Ronson advertisement. TOP RIGHT: Marilyn Monroe wears the button-front Rose Marie Reid swimsuit. BOTTOM LEFT: This Rose Marie Reid suit in satin brocade features box-pleated bloomers. OPPOSITE LEFT: Rose Marie Reid fitting her button-front suit on a model. OPPOSITE RIGHT: Rose Marie Reid drapes fabric on a model during a fitting.

enthusiast. However, these knits can stretch 75 to 90 percent of their original size, whereas Lastex would be closer to 25 percent stretch—a huge difference in fit and effect on the body, but also in the way the pattern needs to be drafted. I found that layering the swimwear spandex with heavy power net (a firm knit usually used in foundation garments like girdles) meant that I was able to retain the convenience of the outer fabric while gaining more stability and control. This layered combo fabric had around 35 percent stretch, making it neither modern nor vintage, but a necessary compromise between the two.

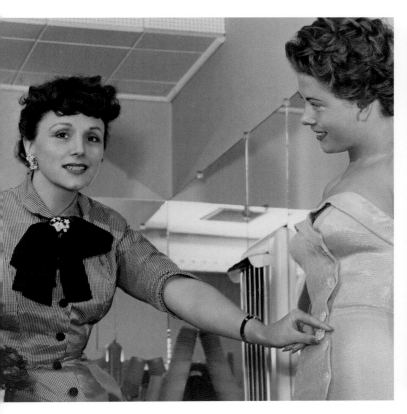

THE DESIGN

With the fabric question solved, I was finally able to turn my attention to the actual design process. (This was a rare occasion where the fabric decision absolutely had to come first, as the pattern could not have been drafted without that crucial stretch percentage number.) Looking at my (now extensive) collection of vintage swimsuits, as well as vintage swimwear photos, ads, and sewing patterns, I knew my top priority would be re-creating the interesting seaming on fifties swimsuits.

Suits of this era often created their shaping through horizontal bust cup seams (which were frequently accentuated in contrast colors or ruched or ruffled details) which then gave way to vertical torso panels (much like the panels on a dress or coat). Rose Marie Reid in particular made use of a dropped waistline to elongate the midsection, with a *basque waistline* that flared out into bloomers on the bottom.

In my sketch, I replicated this vertical paneling on the front of the suit with horizontal upper bust cups and a dropped basque waist, but that's where the similarities to vintage suits had to end. The back of the suit was a real challenge, since a high back (which would have been an authentic vintage look) was impossible to re-create in a fabric with as little stretch as I was using without a zipper. While the high back and firm fabric created an amazing silhouette, it also made it impossible to pull the suit over one's hips! In the studio, we made one maddening attempt to install a zipper into the layers of spandex and power net before admitting defeat. In the end, I turned to a modern-vintage hybrid solution: a bra back combined with a series of hooks and eyes at the lower back. While this created a cutout look on the back that was (dare I say?) trendy, the bra back also engineered amazing bust support, and the hooks and eyes gave a cinched waist.

any girl can be
beautiful and new

Jantzen
best of all swim suits

TOP LEFT: I wanted to re-create the bust seaming similar to this Jantzen suit in my Charm design.
TOP RIGHT: We always review tons of fabric swatches before choosing the one that is just right. OPPOSITE
OPPOSITE: A Rose Marie Reid suit from my collection; this style was worn by both Marilyn Monroe and Jane Russell.

For bottoms, I absolutely wanted to have an array of options, with the bloomers being my own personal favorite and yet another challenge. Studying the bloomers on some Rose Marie Reid Lastex suits in my collection, I was surprised to find they were somewhat complex, and not at all like typical bloomers, which are usually shorts that are *slashed and spread* to create fullness through gathering at the waist and leg openings. Instead, these bloomers had back *princess seams* that were ruched with elastic, and then the side seams had a series of pleats that seemed to go every which way, creating a satisfying puff of fullness in the silhouette. I tried to create something similar and quickly found out it was a lost cause in modern spandex. Pleats and

seams that work well in stable fabrics can be disastrous in slinky knits because they don't have the structure needed to hold up to those shape-building design elements and can just hang sadly instead—the last thing anyone wants in a swimsuit! After several failed attempts at an authentic bloomer re-creation, I cut my losses and tried a simple but classic gathered bloomer instead, omitting power net from the bloomers to reduce bulk. (I also included a simple panty-style bottom, a skirt, and a ruched bottom option.) The result was not what Rose Marie Reid would have done, but it created the silhouette in modern materials—a prime example of how vintage inspiration often plays out in today's real world.

ENGINEERING INNER STRUCTURE

As far as interiors were concerned, I had two goals. First was making the torso as firm and structured as possible, and second was to create bust support. The first goal was achieved through the power net *underlining* (which completely changed the *hand* of the spandex fabric), but I knew that some boning would be required for additional structure.

Yet another obstacle presented itself: Would spiral steel boning work for swimwear? It's a common misconception that steel boning will immediately rust if exposed to water, even just for hand washing. The truth is that spiral steel boning is treated with a coating that will resist rust, so it's no problem to hand wash (or even machine wash on delicate!) your handmade boned dresses. But I wasn't sure how that coating would hold up to the kind of prolonged exposure that a swimsuit

might get if used for actual swimming (not just glamorous poolside lounging, as many designer suits from the mid-century seem to be made for). In the interest of fashion and science, I did a little experiment in the studio: I submerged a spiral steel bone into a cup of water and left it there for two weeks. Half the bone was dipped in the water, and the other half was sticking out of the top of the cup so that I could very scientifically observe the difference in the coating after extended submersion. I chose two weeks because it just seemed like such a ridiculous amount of time to be in the water nonstop that it would (hopefully) prove beyond a shadow of a doubt that spiral steel boning was safe for swimming.

After two weeks, I took the bone out of the water and dried it, letting it sit in the open air for a few more days. While I could observe a slight textural difference in the two halves of the bone (the submerged side felt more rough, while the non-submerged side had a smoother feel), there was no sign of rust or discoloration. Of course, this was a pretty casual experiment and there's no telling how the boning would hold up over years or even decades (not that other elements of a swimsuit hold up that long either!), but it seemed a promising sign that spiral steel boning is much more durable than people think. Buoyed by my experiment, I first added spiral steel bones to the side seams of the suit, which were actually diagonal seams that wrapped around the body, creating a corseted effect.

The next structure to consider was the inner bra. All the vintage swimsuits in my collection have some sort of shelf bra inside the suit (remember this was before the days of molded cups like you find in a modern T-shirt bra), made of the suit material and reinforced with Pellon and vertical bones over the cups. To re-create this type of support, I added a two-piece lower bra cup to the pattern that could be sewn together with the outer, upper horizontal cup to form an inner bra. Instead of papery Pellon, I chose a more modern solution for reinforcing the cups: swimwear foam, which can be purchased by

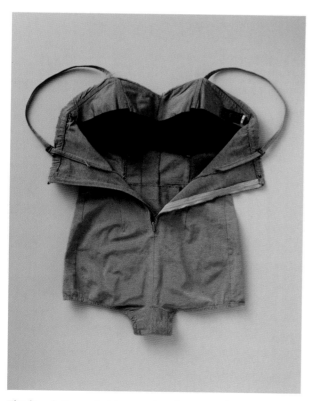

The foundations of vintage swimsuits were often highly structured.

Making Foam Bra Cups

This technique can be used with swimwear foam (also called foam laminate) for bathing suits; however, you can use the same steps for any garment with cups—in this case, you will want to use thin cotton quilt batting rather than foam. These cups can be sewn into your suit or garment, giving permanent structure, support, and coverage. This method works with a two-piece or three-piece cup.

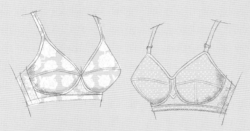

1. Trace your cup pattern pieces and draw in the seamlines with a clear gridded ruler. Trim away the seam allowances by cutting along the marked seamlines.

2. Cut the pattern pieces out in your foam or batting.

3. At the sewing machine, butt the edges of the pieces together and use a wide zigzag stitch to attach them to each other, centering the zigzag over the seam.

The pieces will start to curve into cups as you sew them—like magic! Stitch the cups together at their center front seam.

4. Place the foam cup unit onto the wrong side of the corresponding garment where it will be sewn. (For swimwear, it will likely be into your inner bra cups, and for a garment, you can choose to baste the foam cups to your outer garment unit or to the lining.) Pin the pieces together and stitch around the outer rim of the foam cups, right next to the edge. Now the foam and fabric units are one!

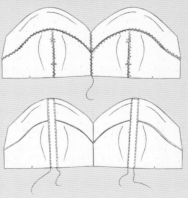

MGM's Queen of COLOR BY TECHNICOLOR Musicals!

Neptune's Daughter

ESTHER WILLIAMS
RED SKELTON

With a Great Cast of Stars! Bathing Beauties! Songs and Spectacle

RICARDO MONTALBAN
BETTY GARRETT
KEENAN WYNN
XAVIER CUGAT *and his orchestra*

Hit Tunes From NEPTUNE'S DAUGHTER Available on M-G-M RECORDS

SCREEN PLAY BY DOROTHY KINGSLEY
ADDITIONAL DIALOGUE BY RAY SINGER AND DICK CHEVILLAT
Directed by EDWARD BUZZELL · Produced by JACK CUMMINGS · A METRO-GOLDWYN-MAYER PICTURE

the yard and sewn into cups using your pattern pieces (see page 113). Then, I added vertical boning channels to the cups for bust shaping and support. Bonus tip: To get a pointy bullet bra look, lightly bend the bones at the bust *apex*.

ABOVE: Esther Williams was known as the "Million Dollar Mermaid." OPPOSITE: Esther Williams in a metallic swimsuit with a petal-like bust.

THE MILLION DOLLAR MERMAID

When it came to naming this swimsuit pattern, there could be no other inspiration than the iconic bathing beauty Esther Williams. Williams was known as the Million Dollar Mermaid and starred in dozens of films featuring the most insanely over-the-top synchronized swimming routines. Truly unhinged displays of unfettered spectacle, these scenes could involve colored volcanic smoke effects, waterskiing men in loincloths waving flags, swimmers in

bejeweled suits diving off swings in unison, fireworks being launched out of the water, and, at the center of it all: Esther, a former champion swimmer, doing daredevil aquatic stunts while dressed in a rhinestoned swimsuit or Greek goddess–inspired swim costume. Her scenes and costumes became more and more outlandish, and in 1952 she broke her neck doing a high dive from a fifty-foot platform in a sequined bodysuit and an ill-advised crown. The impact of the crown snapped her neck and she ended up spending six months in a body cast.

Stretch Percentage and Why It Matters

When a pattern calls for a stretch fabric, using a fabric with the same amount of stretch is crucial to getting the intended fit for the garment. If your fabric has more stretch than intended for the design, your garment will be baggy and lack control. If your fabric has less stretch than intended, your garment will be too tight. A good sewing pattern will tell you the correct stretch percentage you should be looking for in your fabric.

When shopping for fabric online, you'll see that most product descriptions will list the amount of stretch in the fabric so that you don't have to guess. If you're lacking that information from either the pattern company or the fabric seller, you can glean it from these recommended fabrics instead:

- Does the pattern call for things like four-way spandex? That means you're looking for a high amount of stretch, roughly 75 percent.

- If the pattern recommends jersey and interlock, then you're looking at around 50 percent.

- If the pattern calls for ponte, French terry, or stable knits, look for fabrics with around 25 percent stretch.

- Anything under 25 percent will fall into the category of stretch wovens: woven fabrics like denim that have a small amount of spandex blended into them.

To test a fabric's stretch percentage, take 4 inches (10 cm) of the fabric in your hands and stretch as far as possible. If the fabric stretches to 5 inches (13 cm), it has 25 percent stretch. 6 inches (15 cm) means 50 percent stretch, and 7 inches (18 cm) means 75 percent stretch. You can experiment with using a different fabric stretch percentage than recommended, but you will need to adjust the fit of the pattern or size up or down.

ABOVE: As always, Hattie is a star. OPPOSITE, FROM TOP: Original sketch of the Esther Swimsuit; a finished Esther Swimsuit in sweet pink polka dots.

Esther Swimsuit

Esther Williams's movies are such a notable part of pop culture lore and have defined our image of the mid-century bathing beauty in a shapely swim sheath, so of course I wanted to name the Charm suit after her. Instead of sequins, however, I decided on a rainbow theme for the photo shoot. We were set to release the Esther Swimsuit in June. In a nicely timed turn of events, my friend Nathaly Aguilera (who has a pinup hair flower business, La Casa de Flores) proposed a collaboration for LGBTQ+ Pride Month: She wanted to make a series of rainbow flower crowns. I took it a step further and suggested we do not just a traditional rainbow pride scheme but a crown in some of the major pride flag color schemes (pansexual, lesbian, nonbinary, transgender, and bisexual) and then hire a diverse group of models from the communities that the flags represent. This shoot fully embodied what "vintage style, not vintage values" represents to me as a queer person: the ability to separate the fashion of this time from outdated norms of modesty, racism, and heteronormativity.

ESTHER'S DEBUT

In the end, while I love what we created for the photo shoot, I can't exactly call Esther an unmitigated triumph. While the process to design it was slow and laborious, the consumer judgment was instantaneous. It turns out that most modern

The Pride-themed photo shoot for the Charm Patterns Esther Swimsuits.

women balk at the idea of bloomers in swimsuits. (I stand by them to the death!) And then there were so many compromises that had to be made between vintage and modern, making some details overly fussy, perhaps. However, I'm still proud of how much shape and structure we were able to achieve using only modern materials! If I were to design another swimsuit, I think I would pick a camp: either a totally modern swimsuit that has some vintage style lines, or a fully cotton playsuit that could be completely authentic to its time without any restraints placed upon it due to fabric availability.

The Jane Set

After spending a good amount of time in the vintage community, you start to pick up on the "holy grail" fashion items: the ones people would pay a small fortune for and commit minor crimes to obtain in their size. The Ceeb of Miami jumpsuit stands out among these items for its uniqueness, its rareness, and the high price tags it draws. In a sea of poofy dresses, the sleek Ceeb jumpsuit is a totally different animal: a skintight, very stretchy catsuit with a boned bodice and curve-hugging capri-length pants. Think Olivia Newton-John in her bad-girl transformation moment, eschewing the chiffon petticoats and hairbows of her Sandra Dee days.

Ceeb of Miami was (and still is!) a swimsuit manufacturer established in 1942. It's hard to find a lot of history on their jumpsuits, other than a grainy photo showing four models wearing embellished jumpsuits and flat sandals, and an amazing photo of the legendary Black guitar player Barbara Lynn wearing a sequined gold metallic version. Most versions were black or white and featured *soutache* or metallic novelty embellishments like martini glasses or dice trailing down the side of the garment. The more rare the embellishment, the higher the price tag, with jumpsuits often going for $2,000 or more.

I was lucky enough to borrow a Ceeb jumpsuit from a costume rental shop and learned that these jumpsuits were made of Lastex faille, the same material used to make swimsuits, so they had a highly stretchy but firm feeling to them. To make a garment that was so skintight yet meant not for the beach, but for everyday wear, was pretty radical for the time. (We're now used to seeing all manner of body-con garments.) The jumpsuit had an entire boned bra and a back metal zip, and it conformed to my body like a glove when I tried it on. I knew I had to re-create it for Charm.

Much like with the Esther Swimsuit, the biggest obstacle was finding the right fabric. Luckily, there are so many stretch wovens out there these days that I was able to get a close approximation with stretch bengaline (a ribbed synthetic suiting fabric) and techno stretch wool (a four-way stretch woven fabric with a whopping 8 percent elastane blended in).

The pattern became the Jane Set, named for Jane Russell in *Gentlemen Prefer Blondes* (my all-time favorite movie!). Incorporating the interior structure and getting to experiment with trims and appliqués in such a whimsical way was a super-freeing design challenge.

ABOVE: **Ceeb of Miami manufactured structured swimsuits and cabana sets but is now mostly famous for their over-the-top embellished stretch jumpsuits made of Lastex fabric.** NEAR RIGHT: **Examples of embellishment on two Ceeb jumpsuits.** FAR RIGHT AND OPPOSITE: **The Charm Patterns Jane Set.**

6

The Cummerbund Bubble Dress

In 1959, the Wards catalog (formerly known as Montgomery Ward) published a lovely floral taffeta dress in their Junior Fashion Shop. It was worn by a smiling young model with short brunette hair, looking exceptionally wholesome while holding a teacup and wearing white gloves. The copy read as follows:

> *Romantic Rustlings of a flower-strewn print in crisp, whispering Acetate Taffeta tells so many nice things about you! Intricate draping of a newly shaped cummerbund narrows your waist as it circles to a large bow and fishtail-effect back interest. Billowing skirt poufs out to a harem hem, in a skirt interlined with Nylon Net. Dress Acetate Taffeta lined. Back zip. Color: Blue with turquoise and lilac on white ground only. Dry Clean.*
>
> *Junior sizes: 7, 9, 11, 13, 15.*
> *Ship wt. 2 lbs. 2 oz.*
>
> *DA 8048–State size 16.98*

OPPOSITE: The Charm Patterns Betty Dress, an homage to a 1959 dress from the Wards catalog, shown here in embroidered dupioni with an iridescent taffeta cummerbund and bow.

What I love about this description is that you can practically hear what the dress would sound like as you wore it! Taffeta is one of my favorite fabrics, and it certainly does whisper and rustle, thanks to its crispness. The "harem hem" is what we now (thankfully) call a "bubble hem," which folds under the dress's bottom and attaches to the lining underneath, forming a bouffant shape. The "newly shaped" cummerbund was a ruched overlay in solid taffeta, creating a beautiful hourglass shape at the waist and upper hips. Whatever the "large bow and fishtail-effect back interest" looked like would have to be in the imagination of the Wards catalog reader, as no back image is included. In the age of online shopping, with all of its information, it's pretty wild to imagine ordering a dress for $16.98 (roughly $170 in today's money) without even knowing what the back of it looks like, especially when things like large bows and fishtail effects can go horribly awry in the wrong hands.

I happen to have this issue of the Wards catalog in my possession, and this style certainly caught my eye amid the other "Glamour Time Lovelies" in the junior department. Its delicate floral bouquets on white stood out among the dark solid dresses in the fall/winter collection. It is clear that 1959 was a time for cummerbunds in juniors' formal wear, with several of the dresses featuring beautifully shaped midriffs—though none quite as lovely as the floral dress in question.

THE *MAD MEN* EFFECT

The Wards dress is one of those designs that might have been destined for complete obscurity had it not been for the intervention of the 2007 pop culture phenomenon *Mad Men*. The character Betty Draper wore this dress (or a version of it—there are some slight variations between the Wards catalog image and the one actress January Jones wore as Betty) in episode 2 of season 1, entitled "Ladies Room."

Costume designer Janie Bryant sourced many authentic vintage garments for the TV show rather than having them all built from scratch based on vintage inspiration, and she likely sourced this dress from a vintage seller or a rental house. (Incidentally, the same dress appeared in 2019 on an extra in the TV show *The Marvelous Mrs. Maisel* more than a decade later, spotted by an astute Tumblr called *Recycled Movie Costume*s.) In any case, it was the perfect dress for the character in this episode. Betty was a housewife with two children, but her wearing a dress from the juniors department made so much sense—her infantilization and childlike nature are recurring themes in the series. Betty looks like a Grace Kelly clone in this episode, with her coral lips and matching nails. Her jewelry is perfectly fifties: a matching costume necklace and earrings set in bright blue. She carries a beaded clutch, and the dress certainly swishes and rustles as she walks.

Since the release of *Mad Men*, this particular dress has kept popping up on Pinterest and for

sale on Etsy. Heralded as the iconic Betty Draper dress, it's astounding to see how many different color and print combinations it was produced in! There's the version that Betty wore: a blue and pink floral bouquet with a Cinderella blue cummerbund and bow. But then you'll also see the same floral with different sashes: pink, green, and even lavender. There's a green floral version with a pink cummerbund and a straight (rather than bubble) hem, and a white organza version with red embroidery and a red cummerbund. As my search continued, I found some in color-blocked solids, with the upper bodice in deep butterscotch velvet and the cummerbund and skirt both in a lighter dusty yellow taffeta, creating a monochromatic effect.

It's uncertain if Wards created all these versions, but it's clear that this style captured the attention of fashion consumers in the late fifties. Why was this dress so special, so often repeated? My first hunch is that the fabric combinations struck a chord with their garden party florals and shimmering taffetas in candy tones. Secondly, I think the silhouette was both intensely of the moment and somewhat new. (Remember that "newly shaped cummerbund" from the copy?) Instead of a simple banded cummerbund, this one played with angles and created a cinched princess-like look with ruching in style lines that brought to mind a corset or *basque waist*. Meanwhile, the bubble hem foreshadowed the bouffant styles that would become popular in the next decade. And that bow was unlike any I've seen in any dress since (more on that later). No wonder this design was so popular and continues to captivate vintage lovers today.

CREATING A DAPPER VERSION

After seeing this dress pop up periodically for the past fifteen years, I became fixated on re-creating a version for myself. One of my great pleasures in sewing is occasionally making an over-the-top dress for myself without thinking about how to create it for the sewing market. Of course, the irony is that sometimes these projects become part of Charm's lineup—but I allow myself not to think about that as I sew them! Some of Charm's best work has come about this way, and the Betty Dress is no exception. So, I decided that I absolutely needed to re-create this dress for a trip to Disneyland for Dapper Day.

Dapper Day is my favorite vintage style event: a couple of days at Disney parks around the world for vintage fashion enthusiasts to dress up in elevated retro style and gather together at the Happiest Place on Earth. The founder of Dapper Day, Justin Jorgensen, has been quoted as saying he came up with the idea after seeing the original 1954 concept art for Disneyland, complete with visitors dressed in their Sunday best. "I thought as an aside one day, 'Wouldn't

ABOVE: The original bubble hem dress was featured in the juniors section of the 1959 Wards catalog. OPPOSITE, FROM LEFT: This dress is highly coveted and often fetches high prices on vintage resale sites.

it be funny if we could actually make this come to life?'" Jorgensen said in a 2015 interview. "The illustrations that the Imagineers made, all of that became real, all the buildings became real. It was just the guests, over time, that turned into a different sort of visual."

It's true that early visitors to Disneyland, which opened in 1955, treated a day at the park as an occasion to look their best. Women wore dresses and heels, men wore suits or trousers and ties, and children wore church clothes or elevated

A hatbox still packed from one of my many visits to Dapper Day.

play clothes. Given how much that has changed in modern times (I went to last year's Christmas party at Disney World, and many families' versions of festive dress were matching pajamas!), it's easy to see why vintage enthusiasts would be so taken with the original concept art. The idea of true fifties fashion against the magical backdrop of the parks is an image too great to resist for many of us (especially those who are also equally entranced with all things Disney).

And so, at least once a year, I make the pilgrimage to Dapper Day in either Anaheim or Orlando, armed with a suitcase of newly sewn dresses and hats, gloves, parasols, and coordinating jewelry and shoes (usually flats, I admit). It's a beloved tradition to stroll the parks in one's vintage best, calling "Happy Dapper Day!" to kindred spirits. This activity all causes much confusion to the park's usual guests in their T-shirts and shorts, and it's another tradition to have to explain what Dapper Day is to these befuddled masses. The beauty of the occasion is that there isn't one—no meetups or events (outside of a vintage shopping expo at the Disneyland Hotel in Anaheim), just the experience of promenading down Main Street, U.S.A., with like-minded folks and seeing people in vintage finery, as Walt himself had envisioned. Some Dapper Day guests use the opportunity to create character-themed outfits (called Disneybounding to those in the know). However, my personal favorite is to see guests in beautiful true vintage or handsewn ensembles, with no theme other than to be fabulous. The vintage sewing community comes out in full force for Dapper Day, and we take preparations very seriously.

So for a spring Dapper Day in Anaheim, I put together a Pinterest board for potential outfits to make, complete with possible fabrics, trims, and accessories. I wanted florals for spring (groundbreaking) and over-the-top vintage femininity. The Betty Draper Wards dress kept coming up in my inspiration images, and I knew it was time to tackle the pattern.

The Charm Patterns Betty Dress in silk
organza with a taffeta cummerbund

MAKING THE BETTY PATTERN

While sometimes I am lucky enough to be able to
purchase the vintage pieces I'm inspired by, often
budget and lack of supply keep me from being able
to add to my inspiration collection. The Wards
dress was one of those instances, as this vintage
dress is so coveted that it is always snapped up
quickly at pretty high prices. So instead, I started
by finding every photo I could of the dress. I hope
my approach to drafting the Betty Dress can give
you some pointers for re-creating a vintage dress
from a photo or fashion illustration.

Tips for Copying Vintage Details from a Photo

Much like I did with the Betty Dress, it's very possible to reproduce a vintage garment with only photos or video to guide you. It just requires a little sleuthing!

Study the garment as closely as you can, looking for the following:

- **How is the shaping achieved?** Look for princess seams, darts, or bust gathers so that you can start with the best pattern to mimic the vintage garment's fit.

- **Try to imagine the fabric.** How does it feel? Is it stretchy or rigid? Soft and slinky or structural and crisp? Using the right fabric is half the battle.

- **What does the armhole look like?** I'm often asked if a sleeve can be added to a sleeveless dress, or if a *set-in sleeve* style can be added to a *raglan* blouse. Understanding how sleeves are drafted will help you understand what is possible with the patterns in your collection.

- **What are the key design elements and how might they be drafted and sewn?** With the Betty Dress, it was easy to see that the cummerbund was the star of the show. I had to take clues from how it fit and how the edges sat on the dress below to determine how it was drafted and sewn (i.e., was it seamed in? Or was it an overlay?)

- **Research.** Once you have some clues to the construction process, spend time with resources that can help you understand how to make your vision come to life. I like to look at my favorite patternmaking and sewing books, and study similar dresses on Pinterest.

- **Sketch.** Take all your new found knowledge and theories and see what happens when you put it on paper. Sketching helps me with the process of understanding the fine details of a project.

- **Consult your pattern library.** What patterns do you own that can help you achieve the look you want? New patterns are very rarely started entirely from scratch, and you probably can use something similar in your collection as a starting point.

Studying photos of vintage dresses is a great way to understand construction and fashion history better. Thank goodness for the tireless (and often thankless) work of vintage sellers, who take museum-worthy photos of garments on dress forms. While they can only sell the piece once, these photos end up on sites like Pinterest and Tumblr in perpetuity. Looking at pictures of the taffeta Wards dress, I could see that it would be reasonably easy to devise an approach that would mimic the lines of the dress in a satisfactory way, even if the construction wasn't wholly authentic to the original.

Looking at the bodice, I saw a relatively simple *block* with bust and waist darts, a rounded neck that was neither too high nor too low, and a V-back. Many fifties dresses start with this basic idea and then add embellishments, and this one is an excellent example of that. I came up with a plan to start with my favorite block (similar to the one used in the Night and Day Dress from Chapter Two) and add the cummerbund, yoke, and skirt details from there.

The big questions were how to draft the yoke and how the cummerbund was attached. The unusual thing about this cummerbund (and the thing that makes it so beautiful) is that it doesn't end at the waist. It begins below the bust, continues over the waist, and becomes a skirt yoke shaped over the hips. The skirt releases in densely packed gathers from there. While I could have used a hip-length *sloper* shaped with *fisheye darts*, I always feel like I get better waist shaping with a sloper with a waistline seam. So I decided that the cummerbund would be an overlay that concealed the waistline seam and separate yoke underneath. But how would it attach to the bodice?

Doing some finishing work by hand on a silk organza Betty Dress.

In photos, it looked like the lower edge of the cummerbund was seamed together with the skirt. But the upper edge looked to be floating on top. In the end, I decided on a simple solution of turning in the upper edge of the cummerbund and having it lie on top of the dress, seamed in at the side seams and back zipper and tacked at the center front with a few hidden hand stitches.

To draft the yoke, I used the top of a fitted skirt block, omitted the darts, and drew in the lovely tulip shape of the yoke.

The cummerbund came next. I knew from experience that this piece would need to be tested several times—as the crowning jewel of the dress, it needed to be perfect. This type of pattern piece can be deceptive to draft, as it defies common sense. It follows the silhouette of the dress, but it can't be a mere cookie-cutter outline of the dress pieces. It needs to cinch and pull tautly over the dress so that the ruching is "snatched" instead of bagging out unbecomingly. I figured the cummerbund would possibly need to make use of the *bias grain* and be cut smaller than the dress itself, so that it

would stretch over the body to create a beautiful hourglass shape. After drafting the base shape of the cummerbund front and back by combining the bodice and yoke at the waist, I drafted the ruching by *slashing and spreading*, experimenting with different gathering ratios. Then, I shaved width from the sides of the pieces, gradually testing at various stages to get the exact right shape and size. This experimentation is what I love about the pattern process—starting with a theory, and then testing and retesting until it comes out the way you intended.

The skirt was simpler to draft but required a game plan. Typically, a gathered skirt is a simple rectangle, but this one would need to be shaped to reflect the hip yoke. The bubble skirt construction also involved a series of decisions. I ended up drafting a separate A-line skirt to line the bubble skirt, which eliminated the need for gathers at the waist and was the anchoring point for the bubble skirt hem.

THE FISHTAIL BOW

As I studied images of the vintage dress, I could see the bow and "fishtail-effect back interest" in dozens of photos—and frustratingly, it still eluded me. The top of the bow (the "bunny ears" part) was fairly typical, with a lovely cascading shape. In patternmaking, cascades are achieved through circular or spiral slashing and spreading, so I knew I could take a rectangular bow shape and adjust it for circular fullness. It was the tails of the bow that eluded me. They extended to the hem of the dress in an oddly pleasing, extended dagger-like triangular shape. Instead of being two separate pieces, as bow tails would typically be, it was one piece with a seam down the center. Though a little bizarre, there was something strangely beautiful

TOP LEFT: **My first attempt to understand the bow by testing a quick drape in half scale.** BOTTOM LEFT AND OPPOSITE: **The Charm Patterns Betty Dress in silk organza with a taffeta cummerbund.**

ABOVE: **Susie in a Betty Dress muslin, with the cummerbund and bow made in silk taffeta to mimic the drape of the final fabric.**

about this odd bow shape that raised the dress from juvenile to couture.

I started by trying to *drape* the bow in half scale, which is a great way to test small pieces or design elements. I hand-cut a very rough, weird arrowhead/stingray shape with a slash down the top for gathering and wrapping the bow knot around. I cut it on the bias to encourage the flouncing of the bow and used *dupioni* to mimic the drape of the silk I would be using for the dress. The result was not encouraging. With only a day left before I left for Disneyland (who doesn't love stress sewing?!), I decided to take a more traditional approach with the bow by creating the usual rectangular center and knot and a long tie piece with slanted ends. Though

it was cute, it was not the bow of my dreams—or the vintage original.

Once I decided to make this pattern available through Charm, I was excited to have the opportunity to spend more time with the bow conundrum. I collaborated with the Charm team and devised a new tactic. Andrea, Charm's production manager, made the offhand comment that perhaps the bow was seamed into the skirt's center back seam. Eureka! It seems so obvious now, but that was the missing piece of the puzzle. Through trial and error, we came up with a bow shape that was stitched into the skirt, had circular fullness at the top, and a slit for the knot to pass through. Underlined with stiff net, the bow has a lovely shape. What a journey!

CHOOSING A FABRIC

One of the most challenging parts of re-creating a vintage dress is finding suitable fabrics, especially

Fabrics for Testing Patterns

At Charm, we make most of our tests in *muslin*, or unbleached cotton fabric in a medium weight. It is unforgiving, showing every wrinkle and bump, which is what you want when looking at fit with a critical eye. However, there are times when you'll want to select a different fabric for testing. For example, knit patterns must always be tested in a knit. For the Betty Dress, we tested the bodice and skirt in muslin but always tested the cummerbund in silk taffeta. Taffeta had the crispness the dress called for, and also provided textural contrast which was helpful in looking at the pattern tests.

I happened to have overbought some yellow silk taffeta online because I fell in love with the name of the color, "Dusted Buttercup." I thought that was just the most lovely, romantic color name I'd ever heard! I was imagining lovely buttercream roses on a cake in muted lemon yellow. When it arrived, it had a distinct greenish cast and almost veered mustard in certain lights. My romantic buttercup dreams dashed, the taffeta was stashed away for another project. It just so turned out that project was testing dozens of ruched cummerbunds for the Betty Dress.

While it's not ideal to spend a lot of money on testing fabric, it can be a great way to use up a fabric you don't love. Even better would be a less expensive version of the fabric you plan to use–so instead of silk taffeta, try an acetate or polyester taffeta. And above all, don't order 8 yards of silk taffeta online just because you like the name of the color!

in a design where the material plays such a central role. The Wards dress was made in a fabric that is virtually unheard of these days: an acetate taffeta with a distinctive bouquet print. While you may find an allover floral (as opposed to clustered bouquets) in taffeta, it is likely to be silk and very expensive. One of my biggest vintage fantasies is being able to go back in time and go fabric shopping! This is why I got into designing my own fabrics, to re-create the feel of vintage fabrics.

However, sometimes you have to work with what you can find in a fabric store, and I'm lucky to have all of New York City's Garment District within a short drive from where I live and work. After many frustrating attempts to find a suitable print online, I went to B&J Fabrics in New York and explored their options. After flipping through every floral print, I ended up in the embroidered-fabrics section (one of my favorite parts of the store). I landed on an ivory embroidered silk *dupioni* with large sprays of purple, pink, and pale yellow flowers in a row along one selvage, graduating up to single small flowers on the opposite selvage. This sort of print layout is known as a border print, a vintage type of fabric design I've spent a lot of my career chasing and re-creating in various ways.

One reason I love border prints is that they present interesting design challenges. While you can always go the most expected route of placing the border design along the hem of a skirt with a straight hem (like a pencil skirt or gathered *dirndl* skirt), you can also flip them around and place the print upside down or even lengthwise along the body. Some border prints even have smaller borders along one selvage that you can orient along a sleeve hem or neckline.

Looking at the embroidered floral dupioni, I almost discounted it because of the bubble hem. A bubble hem has to be longer than a traditional skirt hem, because it doubles back on itself and connects to the lining inside the skirt. And because a border print usually has minimal fabric underneath the border design, the bouquets would end up inside

ABOVE: **The search for the perfect purple taffeta— and the perfect thread to match.** OPPOSITE: **Reviewing swatches in the studio.**

the skirt rather than above the hem. I took a moment to study the yardage—you have to look at the entire motif, *selvage* to selvage, to understand a border print fully. Looking back at the Betty Draper dress, I realized that the most important thing was not to have a row of bouquets around the skirt hem but to place a bouquet front and center on the chest. This could be achieved by turning the fabric upside down and cutting the bodice crosswise on the yardage. Then I could continue the upside-down crosswise layout on the skirt, having the bouquets appear below the waistline seam and then graduate to the single florals and the bubble hem. It would work beautifully and also call to mind the original vintage dress by prioritizing the placement of the bouquets.

The floral fabric was only half the battle! Finding the right solid taffeta for the cummerbund was the next step, and it proved (almost) as challenging as the main fabric. I had

a swatch of purple taffeta in my fabric samples drawer, and it was the perfect color and crispness. I placed an order for it, only to hear back that it was out of stock. Curses! This small misfortune led to a weeks-long series of orders for swatches from various fabric retailers. (It's always a good idea to order swatches when an exact color match is needed.) I agonized over the pile of purple scraps of fabric, which became a sort of running joke in the studio. I was not satisfied with any of them, and none could ever live up to that first perfect purple!

With time running out before Dapper Day, I chose the purple that offended me the least: a taffeta called Purple Ash with magenta and blue threads woven together to form an *iridescent* purple. I hated the name, and as it's been established, names are very important to me regarding fabric colors. The tone seemed too cool, too basic royal purple. I could find nothing but fault in this poor taffeta. When it arrived, I was shocked by how gorgeous and perfect it was—even better than the original one I was so fixated on. As with a messy breakup, sometimes you just need a little time to get over the perfect fabric!

After I completed the pattern, another struggle in constructing the dress was deciding how to add fullness to the bubble hem. Full-skirted dresses are usually given their fifties silhouette through separate petticoats worn underneath the dress, but a bubble hem needs fullness in between the layers of the skirt. In a vintage dress, that would most likely be achieved with stiff crinoline tulle. Because I was on such a tight timeline for Dapper Day, instead of creating a tulle inner structure, I cut the top off of an old petticoat and sewed it inside the dress. This created just the right amount of fluff in a quick and easy way.

CREATING THE CHARM VERSION

After I posted my Disneyland photos of the dress to social media, the response was resounding:

This design needed to be a Charm Pattern. I couldn't agree more! From the time I started drafting the pattern, I knew this style was a perfect match for Charm. It had fashion pedigree, a pop culture angle, oodles of design interest, intriguing construction, and the perfect vintage silhouette. I'd already christened it the Betty Dress in my mind. However, just because the pattern was drafted didn't mean the work was done! For Charm, I typically provide more than just one dress option in a pattern. So I started to brainstorm elements that could be added to the pattern to round it out.

Of course, the easiest variation would be a simple gathered skirt alternative to the bubble hem; that only involved adding a second cutting line higher up on the bubble skirt pattern piece. I wouldn't have initially thought to add a pencil skirt to this pattern, but a commenter on social

ABOVE AND OPPOSITE: **These dresses both feature delicate floral taffeta fabric and cummerbunds in a coordinating solid color.**

The Evolving Language of Fashion

In January 2023, the *New York Times* published an interesting article called "You Can't Say That! (Or Can You?)," about the shifting standards for what is considered offensive language (whether racist, sexist, ableist, transphobic, or other). As they noted, in just a few short years, there had been rapidly changing "rules," and even well-meaning people found it hard to keep up. Similarly, in just the span of my career in the sewing industry, there has been a lot of growth in understanding what fashion words are ready for retirement. By the time this book is published, several new words may have evolved as well! In an enlightened society, I believe we should all welcome this shifting language while refraining from harshly judging those who used these now-offensive words in the past or are still learning. It always surprises me when people want to hold long-deceased designers accountable for things that weren't yet considered problematic. For instance, there was a time when using global motifs and elements in fashion was considered both cool and sophisticated—much of which is now (rightfully) frowned upon for being culturally appropriative. This is progress!

Here are a few examples of currently accepted language (at the time of writing), which has replaced more dated terms:

- **TROPICAL:** This term has replaced "tiki" as a way to describe fashions inspired by vintage beach vacations. Tiki culture is somewhat controversial in its glamorization of colonialism and its kitsch depictions of Polynesian culture (see page 37). Tropical prints and motifs are something we can all enjoy.

- **PATIO DRESS:** A beloved fifties style, this is a Southwestern style of dress developed in Arizona. These fabulous pieces had broomstick pleating and rows of metallic trim, and they are super fun to reproduce at home. The term "patio" replaces a word that is generally considered a slur against Native American women.

- **CUT-ON SLEEVE:** In the fifties, "kimono sleeves" were all the rage. Any sleeve that was cut in one piece with a bodice, like a dolman sleeve or a fitted sleeve with a gusset, was referred to with this term. In the past few years, the use of the word "kimono" to describe anything that is not the traditional Japanese garment has become heavily frowned upon. In this case, it's easy enough to replace the word with the more accurate term: a "cut-on sleeve."

- **DROP-CROTCH OR GATHERED ANKLE PANTS:** There is a lot of glamorization of "harem" or "genie" pants styles in vintage culture, but those terms can veer into tricky territory in terms of both misogyny (glorifying sexual slavery) and exoticism of Eastern cultures (also known as Orientalism). Again, it's quite easy to replace these problematic terms with a more technical approach to describing a garment.

- **BAND COLLAR:** The term "Mandarin collar" has been used historically for any collar that has only the *stand*/band part of a collar, and not the part that folds over the band like a traditional shirt collar. As many Asian elements in Western dress can be seen as cultural appropriation, it is more sensible to use the term "band collar" here, which is free of cultural implications.

Betty Dress
Charm '22

- *full*
  subble
  hem

- *non-subble*
  hem

slit

pencil skirt

ABOVE: My original Betty Dress sketch.
RIGHT AND OPPOSITE: Different fabrics and skirt options for the pattern show its versatility.

media suggested it and I loved the idea—it would provide the perfect grown-up counterpoint to the sweet bubble hem. This more sophisticated vision of Betty needed a sleeve, too, something dramatic and glamorous. I live for a bishop sleeve, and I wanted one that I could take a step further. I added a slit to the outside of the sleeve, showing just a hint of skin.

For the photo shoot, we remade the bow on the purple dress in its new, improved form. We also made new floral versions, one in a rose print organza I'd had in my stash for more than a decade, just waiting for the perfect project. I paired it with an olive green taffeta, an unusual and very vintage combination. We made our house model, Susie, a bubble hem version in a delicate white and navy floral with a coordinating navy cummerbund, and she looked just like a little doll,

This black lace Betty Dress is underlined with blush silk taffeta and utilizes the scalloped selvage of the lace on the sleeve (accented with little rhinestones).

especially when we styled her with white sheer ruffled gloves and a white rose hair flower.

Of course, we had to figure out a feasible way to instruct pattern users to create fullness inside the bubble skirt (other than telling them to hack up an old petticoat and toss it inside the skirt!). We settled on creating a doubled ring of stille crinoline tulle, folded lengthwise so that there was a soft fold at the bottom. The ring is inserted into the seam where the bubble skirt meets the lining, and the rounded shape of the fold fills out the bubble hem.

For the pencil skirt, we made Susie a cheerful polka-dot version in quilting cotton, specifically to show a more economical fabric.

We dressed it up with a cherry red taffeta cummerbund.

I wanted to show Betty in a darker light for the final version. I used a fabulous fishnet lace fabric from the studio stash and layered it over the palest blush taffeta to create a vampy (dare I say lingerie-inspired?) look. The lace had a scalloped design at the border, which I cut around with small scissors to make a shaped edge. I then aligned the scalloped edge with the straight slit

This vintage taffeta dress from my collection has an unusual bubble hem with an asymmetrical layer.

opening edge on the bishop sleeve. After the sleeve was constructed, I tacked a couple of the points of the scallops closed with tiny rhinestone beads. It's like Betty has an older goth sister!

As always, the pattern also went through rigorous testing in the full 2–34 size range after

Scenes from a day in the life of the Charm studio.

the *grading* process. We have two size *blocks*, 2–20 and 18–34, and they both need to be sewn to be checked for any issues that come up in grading. For example, the cummerbund had to be manually adjusted on this dress in each size, since it doesn't correspond 1:1 to the pieces it gets sewn

to. The journey from a photo of a vintage dress to a finished Charm Pattern can be full of surprises, but it's always worth the effort.

Now that you've seen this process on several classic designs, read on to Part Two to see three new patterns come to life--and sew them yourself!

PART TWO

How to Sew the Patterns

Now that you've come along on the journey of designing several vintage-inspired patterns in the Charm archive, we're going to apply those same processes to three all-new patterns. These patterns (the Madeleine Dress, the Camille Sheath, and the Lillian Jacket) are inspired by twentieth-century designers you read about in Part One. They each represent a pattern I've wanted to design for years, and I'm thrilled to offer them here for your sewing pleasure.

ABOVE: Elvira, our studio mouser, takes a much-needed rest on the pattern inventory boxes. OPPOSITE: The Juki industrial machine is my favorite for everyday sewing. PREVIOUS PAGE: Andrea and Kristen hard at work in the Charm Studio.

The Patterns

The three patterns that accompany this book, along with the pattern hacks, are inspired by true vintage classics. They are intermediate-to-advanced designs with some sewing knowledge assumed. While you may be used to paper patterns being included in my books, I felt it was crucial to provide the full Charm size range (one of the most inclusive I know of, with thirty-nine dress sizes and A-H cup sizes for each of those separate sizes!). To allow for so many sizes to be included, we have pivoted to PDF patterns that you can download and print at home or at a copy shop (online or brick-and-mortar). The sewing pattern industry itself is becoming wholly digital, a move that I think would fascinate and enthrall the designers and sewists from my favorite design eras.

The patterns are available for download at Charmpatterns.com/charmedstudio-resources. We've also provided guides and resources to using PDF patterns and to printing economically (independent online copy shops are a wonder and much cheaper than chain copy shops, for instance). You can also choose to print only your size, and only the pattern pieces you require.

SIZING

The patterns come in two independent size ranges: 2 through 20 and 18 through 34, both with A-H cups. This is Charm's own sizing system, and it is similar to American ready-to-wear sizes. Charm's 2–20 range tends to be more generous in the bust and hip than other systems, with more of an hourglass shape. The 18–34 range is designed for more curves everywhere, with a larger waist measurement relative to the bust and hips. Please measure yourself carefully and check the size charts before deciding on a size!

There are finished garment measurements on page 152, which will also help you decide on a size.

It's incredibly rare for any woman to exactly conform to just one size on the chart, and getting a custom fit is part of what makes sewing so satisfying. Don't be afraid to *grade* between sizes or adjust the pattern pieces for your own body.

SEAM ALLOWANCES

All pattern pieces include a ⅝-inch (1.5 cm) seam allowance, unless otherwise noted.

ASSUMED SKILLS & RESOURCES

These patterns and pattern hacks are designed for intermediate to advanced sewists. Instead of including basic sewing skills in this book, I have created step-by-step video tutorials that accompany each pattern. The video tutorials include skills like the clean finish method (to prepare for zipper insertion), understitching, sewing a lapped zipper, creating *bound buttonholes*, and more. You can find those videos, as well as further information, at Charmpatterns.com/charmedstudio-resources.

CHARM PATTERNS SIZE CHART

Not sure which size range to choose? Read more about our two size ranges at
https://charmpatterns.com/introducing-the-new-size-range-for-charm-patterns-and-patreon.

SIZES 2–20

SIZES 2–20	2	4	6	8	10	12	14	16	18	20
High Bust	29 in 73.7 cm	31 in 78.7 cm	33 in 83.8 cm	35 in 88.9 cm	37 in 94 cm	39 in 99 cm	41 in 104.1 cm	43 in 109.2 cm	45 in 114.3 cm	47 in 119.4 cm
Bust A cup	30.5 in 77.5 cm	32.5 in 82.5 cm	34.5 in 87.6 cm	36.5 in 92.7 cm	38.5 in 97.8 cm	40.5 in 102.9 cm	42.5 in 108 cm	44.5 in 113 cm	46.5 in 118.1 cm	48.5 in 123.2 cm
Bust B/C cup	31 in 78.7 cm	33 in 83.8 cm	35 in 88.9 cm	37 in 94 cm	39 in 99 cm	41 in 104.1 cm	43 in 109.2 cm	45 in 114.3 cm	47 in 119.4 cm	49 in 124.5 cm
Bust D/DD cup	32 in 81.3 cm	34 in 86.4 cm	36 in 91.4 cm	38 in 96.5 cm	40 in 101.6 cm	42 in 106.7 cm	44 in 111.8 cm	46 in 116.8 cm	48 in 121.9 cm	50 in 127 cm
Bust F/G cup	33 in 83.8 cm	35 in 88.9 cm	37 in 94 cm	39 in 99 cm	41 in 104.1 cm	43 in 109.2 cm	45 in 114.3 cm	47 in 119.4 cm	49 in 124.5 cm	51 in 129.5 cm
Bust H cup	34 in 86.4 cm	36 in 91.4 cm	38 in 96.5 cm	40 in 101.6 cm	42 in 106.7 cm	44 in 111.8 cm	46 in 116.8 cm	48 in 121.9 cm	50 in 127 cm	52 in 132.1 cm
Waist	24 in 61 cm	26 in 66 cm	28 in 71.1 cm	30 in 76.2 cm	32 in 81.3 cm	34 in 86.4 cm	36 in 91.4 cm	38 in 96.5 cm	40 in 101.6 cm	42 in 106.7 cm
Hips	36 in 91.4 cm	38 in 96.5 cm	40 in 101.6 cm	42 in 106.7 cm	44 in 111.8 cm	46 in 116.8 cm	48 in 121.9 cm	50 in 127 cm	52 in 132.1 cm	54 in 137.2 cm

SIZES 18–34

SIZES 18–34	18	20	22	24	26	28	30	32	34
High Bust	39.5 in 100.3 cm	41.5 in 105.4 cm	43.5 in 110.5 cm	45.5 in 115.6 cm	47.5 in 120.7 cm	49.5 in 125.7 cm	51.5 in 130.8 cm	53.5 in 135.9 cm	55.5 in 141 cm
Bust A/B cup	42.5 in 108 cm	44.5 in 113 cm	46.5 in 118.1 cm	48.5 in 123.2 cm	50.5 in 128.3 cm	52.5 in 133.4 cm	54.5 in 138.4 cm	56.5 in 143.5 cm	58.5 in 148.6 cm
Bust C cup	43 in 109.2 cm	45 in 114.3 cm	47 in 119.4 cm	49 in 124.5 cm	51 in 129.5 cm	53 in 134.6 cm	55 in 139.7 cm	57 in 144.8 cm	59 in 149.9 cm
Bust D/DD cup	44 in 111.8 cm	46 in 116.8 cm	48 in 121.9 cm	50 in 127 cm	52 in 132.1 cm	54 in 137.2 cm	56 in 142.2 cm	58 in 147.3 cm	60 in 152.4 cm
Bust F/G cup	45 in 114.3 cm	47 in 119.4 cm	49 in 124.5 cm	51 in 129.5 cm	53 in 134.6 cm	55 in 139.7 cm	57 in 144.8 cm	59 in 149.9 cm	61 in 154.9 cm
Bust H cup	46 in 116.8 cm	48 in 121.9 cm	50 in 127 cm	52 in 132.1 cm	54 in 137.2 cm	56 in 142.2 cm	58 in 147.3 cm	60 in 152.4 cm	62 in 157.5 cm
Waist	40 in 101.6 cm	42 in 106.7 cm	44 in 111.8 cm	46 in 116.8 cm	48 in 121.9 cm	50 in 127 cm	52 in 132.1 cm	54 in 137.2 cm	56 in 142.2 cm
Hips	48 in 121.9 cm	50 in 127 cm	52 in 132.1 cm	54 in 137.2 cm	56 in 142.2 cm	58 in 147.3 cm	60 in 152.4 cm	62 in 157.5 cm	64 in 162.6 cm

PREVIOUS PAGE: Andrea tests the Lillian Jacket in some cotton twill we had in the studio stash (sometimes tailored garments require a heavier testing fabric than muslin). OPPOSITE: Kristen hard at work reviewing patterns digitally.

Madeleine Dress

The Madeleine Dress was designed to be the perfect *New Look*–inspired dress that would fit perfectly into any vintage-lover's wardrobe. Christian Dior was known for his fit-and-flare silhouettes that took yards and yards of fabric. I've named this dress for his mother, Madeleine Dior, who was said to be one of his biggest influences, inspiring everything from his interest in flowers to his favorite colors to the famous silhouette he became famous for. Madeleine Dior was especially known for her gardening prowess, and her Les Rhumbs gardens at their Granville estate (now the Museé Christian Dior in Normandy) have been lovingly preserved and are studied today as an example of masterful landscape gardening. Madeleine was also an ardent admirer of fashion, and the Belle Epoque silhouettes she wore in Christian's childhood inspired his first collection, in 1947, with their nipped waists and full skirts.

This pattern was not inspired by any one particular example of New Look fashion, but by the body of work that continues to captivate today. One of the challenges of designing full-skirted silhouettes is how large the pattern pieces become, often proving challenging to cut and choose the correct fabric for (directional prints and narrower widths of fabric can be tricky!). I wanted to think about alternative ways to achieve this silhouette, and landed on the idea of pleated gores: these six triangular skirt pieces are inset into the princess and side seams of the dress, creating volume in a dress that would otherwise be quite slim. I also like to think of these gores as petals, inspired by the flowers Madeleine Dior was passionate about. I sewed this Madeleine Dress with the main pieces and the gores in the same fabric, a tri-color *dupioni* with gorgeous striations in my favorite colors of ruby red, blush, and deep pink. However, you can also get adventurous with contrasting fabrics, as shown in the two other versions on the following pages.

FIT NOTES

The Madeleine Dress has a close-fitting bodice with 2½ in (6.4 cm) of ease in the bust and 1 in (0.6 cm) of ease in the waist. The hip measurement is not important when choosing a size, because of the fullness of the skirt.

FABRIC NOTES

We recommend light-to mid-weight fabric with body: Suitable types include faille, poplin, sateen, satin, silk shantung, or taffeta.

SUPPLIES

- Fabric for dress
- Optional contrast fabric for skirt gores
- 10-in by 30-in (25.4 by 76.2 cm) fusible interfacing
- 24-in (56 cm) regular nylon zipper
- 1-in (2.5 cm) or wider firm grosgrain ribbon or waist stay tape cut to your waist measurement plus 1½ in (3.8 cm)
- Two hook-and-bar pairs
- Thread

INSTRUCTIONS

1 Staystitch the bodice front and back necklines and the inner waistline corners (pivoting at waistline circles) of all dress fronts and back (A).

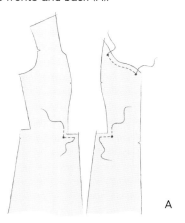

A

2 Stabilize the center back seam allowances with fusible interfacing or fusible stay tape in preparation for inserting the zipper.

3 Turn dress center front skirt pleat underlap 2⅛ inches (5.3 cm) to wrong side, along marked line. Press to crease. Repeat for dress side front, dress side back, and dress center back (B).

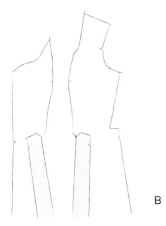

B

4 With right sides together, sew center seam of dress center front from neckline circle to hem.

5 Staystitch center front princess seams between marks. Clip princess seam allowances every ½ inch (1.3 cm), being careful not to clip through stitching. Unfold skirt pleats. Pin dress front to dress side front from neckline to waistline circle, matching circles and spreading clips on front to match curve of side. Stitch, ending and backstitching exactly at the waist circle, and following the pressed crease to the waist circle; do not follow the seam allowance. Notch side front princess seams every ½ inch (1.3 cm), alternating with clips. Clip diagonally into the dress seam allowances at the inner corners above the waist circle. Press seam allowances above clip to center front as one (C).

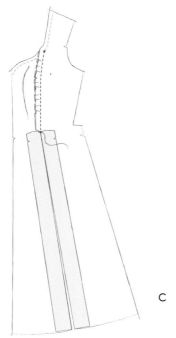

C

6 Sew the back princess seams as for the front.

7 Sew bodice front to bodice back at shoulder seams and side seams (above waistline circle), right sides together.

8 With right sides together, pin dress center front unit to one long side of a skirt gore, matching notches. Stitch long vertical seam of gore only, from waistline to hem. Repeat to attach the opposite side of the gore to the dress side fronts (D).

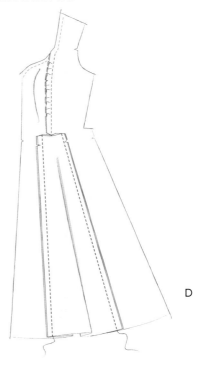

D

9 Repeat the previous step, stitching gores between dress side fronts and dress side backs, and between dress side backs and dress center backs.

10 With right sides together, stitch center back seam from zipper circle to hem. Press seam allowances open.

11 With right sides together, sew front neck facings together at center front.

12 Sew front neck facing to back neck facing at shoulder seams, right sides together.

13 With right sides together, pin facing to the dress neckline, folding the back zipper opening in preparation for inserting a lapped zipper. Stitch around the neckline, folding the center front seam allowances out of the way, and stitching only to the center front seam. Begin stitching on the opposite side of the center front seam, with the seam allowances folded out of the way, and finish the neckline. This will create a perfect sweetheart point at center front. Grade and trim the seam allowances and understitch the facing. Turn the facing to the inside of the dress and press.

14 With right sides together, stitch the sleeve underarm seams.

15 Set the sleeves into the armholes.

16 Form pleats in skirt and pin. Individually baste both sides of each gore to the dress at the waistline horizontal edge (E).

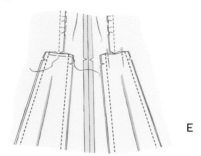

E

17 Insert a lapped zipper.

18 Hand-stitch the facing to the zipper tape.

19 Prepare your waist stay by turning under edges by ¼ inch (6 mm) twice. Stitch the folded edge into place. Form into a ring with ½ inch (1.3 cm) overlap. Sew hooks and bars on either side to fasten it like a belt. Divide the ribbon into quarters and mark center front and sides with a pin.

20 Pin the waist stay to the gores on the inside of the dress, overlapping gores as needed. Place the hook at center back, with the hook on the left side. The bottom edge of the waist stay should align to the waistline. Sew the waist stay to the waistline horizontal seam allowances of each dress/gore section (F).

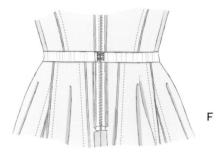

F

21 Let the dress hang for at least twenty-four hours before marking hem. Press skirt gores. Mark the hem of the dress and trim away excess, leaving your desired hem allowance. Hem the skirt using your preferred method, changing thread color as needed for contrast gores. Press hem.

POLKA DOT DAYTIME VERSION

Susie looks so sweet in this cotton daytime version of
the Madeleine Dress! We sewed the body of the dress
in turquoise stretch piqué and then sewed the gores
in coordinating polka-dot broadcloth. Add three tiny
buttons at the center front neckline and some true
vintage accessories and you've got the most darling
day dress ever!

VELVET AND SATIN
COLOR-BLOCKED VERSION

Talk about high glamour! This version was inspired by (yet another) amazing dress that the character Betty Draper wore on the TV show *Mad Men*, a strapless showstopper of a black velvet cocktail dress with satin gores in alternating ivory and shocking pink. I've always wanted to pay homage to that dress, and I knew the Madeleine Dress was the perfect blank canvas for it. The body of the dress is made in black cotton velveteen, and the gores are cut in double-faced silk duchess satin (one of the world's most luxurious fabrics). I added a ginormous satin neckline bow in the bubblegum pink silk for even more drama! To make the bow, cut two rectangles of fabric that are 29 inches by 11 inches (73.7 cm by 27.9 cm) and 5 inches by 5½ inches (12.7 cm by 14 cm). Cut the same rectangles in stiff tulle. Underline the satin rectangles in tulle by basting the two layers together ½ inch (1.3 cm) from the raw edges. To make the bow, sew each rectangle into a tube with right sides together and then turn right side out. Press flat. Form the larger rectangle into a loop and wrap the smaller rectangle around the larger one, pinching the bow in at the center. The smaller rectangle will form the "knot." Hand-stitch the knot in place on the backside of the bow and then tack the bow to the dress by hand at the center front neckline.

FINISHED MEASUREMENTS

Sizes 2–20	2	4	6	8	10	12	14	16	18	20
A-C Bust	33 in / 83.8 cm	35 in / 88.9 cm	37 in / 94 cm	39 in / 99.1 cm	41 in / 104.1 cm	43 in / 109.2 cm	45 in / 114.3 cm	47 in / 119.4 cm	49 in / 124.5 cm	51 in / 129.5 cm
D-G Bust	35.25 in / 89.5 cm	37.25 in / 94.6 cm	39.25 in / 99.7 cm	41.25 in / 104.8 cm	43.25 in / 109.9 cm	45.25 in / 114.9 cm	47.25 in / 120 cm	49.25 in / 125.1 cm	51.25 in / 130.2 cm	53.25 in / 135.3 cm
H Bust	36.25 in / 92.1 cm	38.25 in / 97.2 cm	40.25 in / 102.2 cm	42.25 in / 107.3 cm	44.25 in / 112.4 cm	46.25 in / 117.5 cm	48.25 in / 122.6 cm	50.25 in / 127.6 cm	52.25 in / 132.7 cm	54.25 in / 137.8 cm
Waist	25 in / 63.5 cm	27 in / 68.6 cm	29 in / 73.7 cm	31 in / 78.7 cm	33 in / 83.8 cm	35 in / 88.9 cm	37 in / 94 cm	39 in / 99.1 cm	41 in / 104.1 cm	43 in / 109.2 cm
Hips	71 in / 180.3 cm	73 in / 185.4 cm	75 in / 190.5 cm	77 in / 195.6 cm	79 in / 200.7 cm	81 in / 205.7 cm	83 in / 210.8 cm	85 in / 215.9 cm	87 in / 221 cm	89 in / 226.1 cm
Bicep	12 in / 30.5 cm	12.75 in / 32.1 cm	13.25 in / 33.7 cm	14 in / 35.2 cm	14.5 in / 36.8 cm	15.25 in / 38.4 cm	15.75 in / 40 cm	16.5 in / 41.6 cm	17 in / 43.2 cm	17.75 in / 44.8 cm

Sizes 18–34	18	20	22	24	26	28	30	32	34
A-C Bust	45.5 in / 115.6 cm	47.5 in / 120.7 cm	49.5 in / 125.7 cm	51.5 in / 130.8 cm	53.5 in / 135.9 cm	55.5 in / 141 cm	57.5 in / 146.1 cm	59.5 in / 151.1 cm	61.5 in / 156.2 cm
D-G Bust	47.5 in / 120.7 cm	49.5 in / 125.7 cm	51.5 in / 130.8 cm	53.5 in / 135.9 cm	55.5 in / 141 cm	57.5 in / 146.1 cm	59.5 in / 151.1 cm	61.5 in / 156.2 cm	63.5 in / 161.3 cm
H Bust	48.5 in / 123.2 cm	50.5 in / 128.3 cm	52.5 in / 133.4 cm	54.5 in / 138.4 cm	56.5 in / 143.5 cm	58.5 in / 148.6 cm	60.5 in / 153.7 cm	62.5 in / 158.8 cm	64.5 in / 163.8 cm
Waist	41 in / 104.1 cm	43 in / 109.2 cm	45 in / 114.3 cm	47 in / 119.4 cm	49 in / 124.5 cm	51 in / 129.5 cm	53 in / 134.6 cm	55 in / 139.7 cm	57 in / 144.8 cm
Hips	90 in / 228.6 cm	92 in / 233.7 cm	94 in / 238.8 cm	96 in / 243.8 cm	98 in / 248.9 cm	100 in / 254 cm	102 in / 259.1 cm	104 in / 264.2 cm	106 in / 269.2 cm
Bicep	15.75 in / 40 cm	16.25 in / 41.3 cm	16.75 in / 42.5 cm	17.25 in / 43.8 cm	17.75 in / 45.1 cm	18.25 in / 46.4 cm	18.75 in / 47.6 cm	19.25 in / 48.9 cm	19.75 in / 50.2 cm

PATTERN PIECES

1. **Dress Center Front**
   Cut 2 fabric

2. **Dress Side Front**
   Cut 2 fabric

3. **Dress Center Back**
   Cut 2 fabric

4. **Dress Side Front**
   Cut 2 fabric

5. **Front Neck Facing**
   Cut 2 fabric, 2 interfacing

6. **Back Neck Facing**
   Cut 2 fabric, 2 interfacing

7. **Skirt Gore**
   Cut 6 fabric or contrast fabric

8. **Short Sleeve**
   Cut 2 fabric

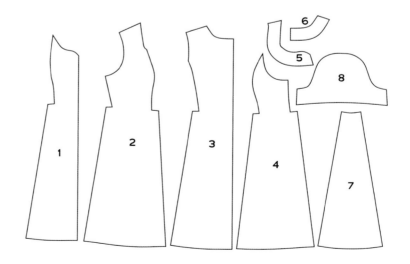

REQUIRED YARDAGE & CUTTING LAYOUTS

Note: All pattern pieces are shown in a "without nap" layout. You may need additional yardage for directional prints, stripes, plaids, and other prints that need to be matched across seamlines.

Fabric (1, 2, 3, 4, 5, 6, 7, 8)

	Sizes 2–10	Sizes 12–20	Sizes 18–34
45 in	5 yds 4.6 m	5½ yds 5 m	5 yds 4.6 m
60 in	3¾ yds 3.4 m	3¾ yds 3.4 m	3¾ yds 3.4 m

KEY TO LAYOUTS

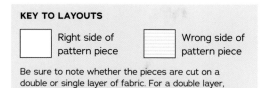

Right side of pattern piece

Wrong side of pattern piece

Be sure to note whether the pieces are cut on a double or single layer of fabric. For a double layer, there will be a note indicating FOLD on the layout.

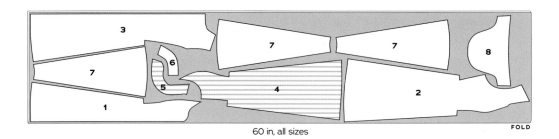

60 in, all sizes

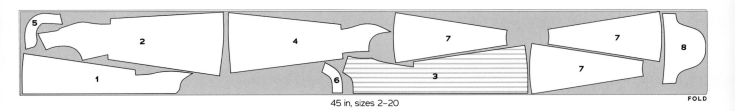

45 in, sizes 2–20

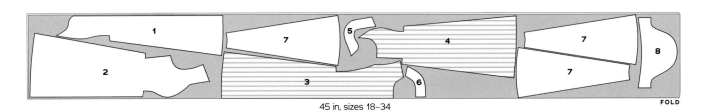

45 in, sizes 18–34

Interfacing (5, 6)

	Sizes 2–20	Sizes 18–34
60 in*	½ yds 5 m	⅜ yd 4.6 m

* Pieces can also be cut from a 10 in by 30 in piece of interfacing.

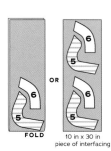

FOLD

OR

10 in x 30 in piece of interfacing

Camille Sheath

This dress was inspired by the work of a designer you read about quite a bit in Part One, Alfred Shaheen. His Shaheen Sheath was one of his most innovative designs, a curvy sheath dress with a softly sculpted pleated neckline. The secret to those beautiful *draped* pleats? Interior lengths of elastic that anchor at the neckline points and get sewn to the back waistline of the dress, forming interior stays that move with the body. Another beautiful feature of this design is the built-up pockets that both are practical (so roomy!) and add to the hourglass shape of the dress. The Camille Sheath looks equally as beautiful in silk brocade or inexpensive tropical print cotton.

I named this homage to the Shaheen Sheath after Alfred Shaheen's daughter, Camille, who has been a wonderful resource to me over the years and an ardent preserver of her father's design legacy. When I first interviewed Camille, she talked about the Shaheen Sheath and its unusual elastic stays. Since elastic degrades over time, original examples of this dress usually have stretched-out stays that can be confused with interior hanging loops. When the stays no longer pull the neckline into pleats, the top of the dress resembles an awkward cowl neck that doesn't sit quite right, with straps that fall off the shoulders. I'm lucky to have two examples of this style in my vintage collection. One is the original pencil skirt style in solid white cotton poplin, while the other is a gorgeous tropical print with tie straps and a full pleated skirt.

Studying those original vintage dresses helped me understand how to draft the pattern for the Camille Sheath.

The neckline of a round-neck *midriff* bodice is *slashed and spread* to create excess fabric, which is then controlled into pleats by the addition of the elastic stays. I highly recommend making a *muslin* of this bodice and testing out the elastic lengths—I've provided suggested measurements, but these will vary depending on your torso length and preferred fit.

Much like the original Shaheen design, the Camille Sheath looks equally beautiful in silk brocade or inexpensive tropical-print cotton. If you'd like to try an authentic Chinese silk brocade, like the fabric I've used here, keep in mind that it comes in very narrow fabric widths (usually only 30 inches wide), so you will need to buy at least twice the recommended yardage.

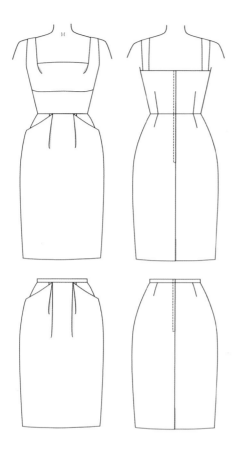

FIT NOTES

The Camille Sheath is a close-fitting dress with ¾ to 2¼ in (1.9 to 5.7 cm) of ease in the bust, ¼ in (.6 cm) of ease in the waist, and ½ to 3¼ in (1.3 to 8.3 cm) the hips.

FABRIC NOTES

We recommend light-to mid-weight fabric with body: Suitable types include poplin, lawn, brocade, faille, sateen, satin, silk shantung, or taffeta.

For the lining, we recommend: broadcloth, lawn, lining fabrics.

SUPPLIES

- Fabric for dress
- Lining fabric
- 1¼-in-wide fusible stay tape to stabilize the pockets amd zipper opening (alternatively, cut strips from a scrap of fusible interfacing yardage)
- 1 yd (.9 m) ¼-in (6-mm) elastic
- 14-in (35.6 cm) regular nylon zipper
- Thread

INSTRUCTIONS

1 Staystitch the bodice front and back necklines.

2 Stitch the darts in the bodice front and back. Stabilize the zipper opening on bodice back with fusible tape applied to the fabric's wrong side.

3 Stitch the bodice front to the midriff. Trim seam allowances and press toward bodice.

4 Sew side seams.

5 Prepare the bodice lining: Sew darts, stitch bodice front to midriff, and sew side seams.

6 Cut two lengths of elastic according to the measurement chart. Working from the right side of the bodice front, pin one end of the elastic to the neckline circle, with the elastic extending to the raw edge of the neckline seam allowance. Repeat for the other length of elastic. Baste into place within the neckline seam allowance (A).

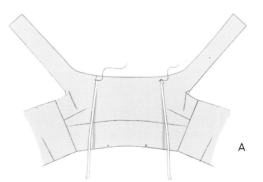

A

7 With right sides together, pin lining to the shoulder strap and neckline, sandwiching the elastic inside and folding the back zipper opening in preparation for inserting a lapped zipper. Stitch the neckline, pivoting at each corner of the shoulder strap. Grade, clip, and trim the seam allowances and understitch the lining. Stitch the short end of the strap and the armhole. Grade, clip, and trim the seam allowances and understitch the lining as far as possible onto the strap. Turn the lining to the inside of the dress and press.

8 Form pleats in skirt front by bringing the pleat lines together, following the arrows on the pattern pieces. Pin and baste along waist seam (B).

B

9 Stitch the darts in the skirt side front and skirt back. Stabilize zipper opening on the skirt backs. With right sides together, stitch the skirt backs together from slit opening to zipper opening notch.

10 Interface top edge of packet bag. Pin skirt pocket bag to diagonal opening on skirt front, right sides together, catching the pleat in the diagonal pocket opening and matching circles on the waistline. Stitch. Grade and trim seam allowances. Understitch pocket bag and press to inside of skirt front.

11 Working from wrong side of skirt, pin pocket bag to skirt side front, right sides together along inner vertical and lower edge. Stitch. Match side seams of skirt front, pocket bag, and skirt side front and baste layers together. Match circle of skirt front, pocket bag, and skirt side front. Baste together at waist.

12 With right sides together, stitch skirt front to skirt backs at side seams.

13 With right sides together, pin the bodice to the skirt, matching side seams, darts, notches, and circles. Stitch bodice to skirt. Trim and grade the seam allowance and press toward bodice.

14 Insert a lapped zipper at center back.

15 Stitch the free end of each length of elastic to the right side of the lining seam allowance at the back dart, being careful not to twist the elastic (C). Press lining waistline seam allowance to wrong side. Stitch lining to dress at waist and zipper by hand. Note: it's a good idea to try on the dress to test the length of the elastic. It should pull the neckline snugly but not be too tight. Adjust the elastic length as needed before finishing the hand stitching at the waist.

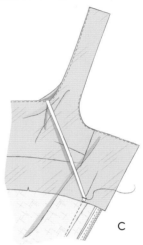

C

16 Try the dress on to determine the strap length and placement. Pin each strap into place on the inside of the dress and stitch to the dress invisibly by hand.

17 Mark the hem of the dress and trim away excess, leaving your desired hem allowance. Hem the skirt and back slit.

OPPOSITE: **The Camille Sheath pairs perfectly with the Charm Patterns Dorothy Bolero (and gorgeous Elvira).**

SCARLET VELVETEEN VERSION

Cotton velveteen is one of my favorite fabrics to sew, and this scarlet version is so glam! We followed the Camille instructions as usual to make Susie's elegant red dress, and we added a gorgeous hair flower worn as a corsage.

TROPICAL PLEATED HACK

Not into slim skirts? It's easy to add a pleated skirt to the Camille Sheath bodice for a fuller look. I also created a tie-shoulder variation, inspired by a vintage Shaheen dress in my collection. Make it in a tropical print cotton and this is the perfect beachy frock.

To make this hack, follow the Camille Sheath instructions as usual, with the following changes:

1 Add 2 ¾ inches (7 cm) to front strap. When sewing the straps, stitch the short ends closed and then turn right side out.

2 Create two 2⅞-inch by 18 ¾-inch (7.3 cm by 47.6 cm) back straps. Fold the straps in half lengthwise and then stitch along the long side and one short end. Turn right side out and press flat. Baste straps to back neckline before attaching the bodice lining. To wear, tie straps into double knots at shoulders.

3 This pleated skirt is just a rectangle! The dimensions are up to you, and depend on your desired amount of fullness, the depth of the pleats you create, and your preferred length. I like my skirts on the longer side, so I made the height of my rectangle 29 inches (73.7 cm) plus seam allowances on the top and botton. For the width, I cut the rectangle about 1.5 times my waist measurement. I then created 1-inch (2.5 cm)–deep pleats all the way around the waistline, starting about 2 inches (5 cm) away from the long vertical sides. I formed my pleats right next to each other, with no space in between. I used a Quick Pleater, a handy tool with fork-like tongs that helps you create uniform pleats as you sew. Compare the skirt waistline to the bodice waistline and remove any excess fabric. To form the skirt center back seam, fold the skirt right sides together and stitch from the lower edge to 7 inches (17.8 cm) away from the waist seam line. Apply strips of fusible interfacing to the seam allowances above the center back seam. Attach this pleated skirt instead of the Shaheen Sheath skirt, and complete the dress as usual.

SKIRT HACK VERSION

I loved the skirt on the Camille Sheath so much, I wanted it as a separate! Make it in wool flannel for the perfect vintage suiting look. We adapted the waistband of the free Charm Circle Skirt (https://charmpatterns.com/charm-circle-skirt) and used a 7-inch (18-cm) zipper. (Alternatively, you can draft your own rectangular waistband.) Attach the waistband to the skirt after the skirt has been assembled and the zipper has been attached.

FINISHED MEASUREMENTS

Sizes 2–20	2	4	6	8	10	12	14	16	18	20
Bust A	32.25 in 81.9 cm	34.25 in 87 cm	36.25 in 92.1 cm	38.25 in 97.2 cm	40.25 in 102.2 cm	42.25 in 107.3 cm	44.25 in 112.4 cm	46.25 in 117.5 cm	48.25 in 122.6 cm	50.25 in 127.6 cm
Bust B/C	32.75 in 83.2 cm	34.75 in 88.3 cm	36.75 in 93.3 cm	38.75 in 98.4 cm	40.75 in 103.5 cm	42.75 in 108.6 cm	44.75 in 113.7 cm	46.75 in 118.7 cm	48.75 in 123.8 cm	50.75 in 128.9 cm
Bust D/DD	33.75 in 85.7 cm	35.75 in 90.8 cm	37.75 in 95.9 cm	39.75 in 101 cm	41.75 in 106 cm	43.75 in 111.1 cm	45.75 in 116.2 cm	47.75 in 121.3 cm	49.75 in 126.4 cm	51.75 in 131.4 cm
Bust F/G	34.75 in 88.3 cm	36.75 in 93.3 cm	38.75 in 98.4 cm	40.75 in 103.5 cm	42.75 in 108.6 cm	44.75 in 113.7 cm	46.75 in 118.7 cm	48.75 in 123.8 cm	50.75 in 128.9 cm	52.75 in 134 cm
Bust H	35.75 in 90.8 cm	37.75 in 95.9 cm	39.75 in 101 cm	41.75 in 106 cm	43.75 in 111.1 cm	45.75 in 116.2 cm	47.75 in 121.3 cm	49.75 in 126.4 cm	51.75 in 131.4 cm	53.75 in 136.5 cm
Waist	24.25 in 61.6 cm	26.25 in 66.7 cm	28.25 in 71.8 cm	30.25 in 76.8 cm	32.25 in 81.9 cm	34.25 in 87 cm	36.25 in 92.1 cm	38.25 in 97.2 cm	40.25 in 102.2 cm	42.25 in 107.3 cm
Hips	39.25 in 99.4 cm	41.25 in 104.5 cm	43.25 in 109.5 cm	45.25 in 114.6 cm	47.25 in 119.7 cm	49.25 in 124.8 cm	51.25 in 129.9 cm	53.25 in 134.9 cm	55.25 in 140 cm	57.25 in 145.1 cm
Center Back Length	36 in 91.4 cm	36.25 in 92.1 cm	36.5 in 92.7 cm	36.75 in 93.3 cm	37 in 94 cm	37.25 in 94.6 cm	37.5 in 95.3 cm	37.75 in 95.9 cm	38 in 96.5 cm	38.25 in 97.2 cm

Sizes 18–34	18	20	22	24	26	28	30	32	34
Bust A/B	43.25 in 109.9 cm	45.25 in 114.9 cm	47.25 in 120 cm	49.25 in 125.1 cm	51.25 in 130.2 cm	53.25 in 135.3 cm	55.25 in 140.3 cm	57.25 in 145.4 cm	59.25 in 150.5 cm
Bust C	43.75 in 111.1 cm	45.75 in 116.2 cm	47.75 in 121.3 cm	49.75 in 126.4 cm	51.75 in 131.4 cm	53.75 in 136.5 cm	55.75 in 141.6 cm	57.75 in 146.7 cm	59.75 in 151.8 cm
Bust D/DD	44.75 in 113.7 cm	46.75 in 118.7 cm	48.75 in 123.8 cm	50.75 in 128.9 cm	52.75 in 134 cm	54.75 in 139.1 cm	56.75 in 144.1 cm	58.75 in 149.2 cm	60.75 in 154.3 cm
Bust F/G	45.75 in 116.2 cm	47.75 in 121.3 cm	49.75 in 126.4 cm	51.75 in 131.4 cm	53.75 in 136.5 cm	55.75 in 141.6 cm	57.75 in 146.7 cm	59.75 in 151.8 cm	61.75 in 156.8 cm
Bust H	46.75 in 118.7 cm	48.75 in 123.8 cm	50.75 in 128.9 cm	52.75 in 134 cm	54.75 in 139.1 cm	56.75 in 144.1 cm	58.75 in 149.2 cm	60.75 in 154.3 cm	62.75 in 159.4 cm
Waist	40.25 in 102.2 cm	42.25 in 107.3 cm	44.25 in 112.4 cm	46.25 in 117.5 cm	48.25 in 122.6 cm	50.25 in 127.6 cm	52.25 in 132.7 cm	54.25 in 137.8 cm	56.25 in 142.9 cm
Hips	48.5 in 123.2 cm	50.5 in 128.3 cm	52.5 in 133.4 cm	54.5 in 138.4 cm	56.5 in 143.5 cm	58.5 in 148.6 cm	60.5 in 153.7 cm	62.5 in 158.8 cm	64.5 in 163.8 cm
Center Back Length	36.75 in 93.3 cm	37 in 93.7 cm	37 in 94 cm	37.25 in 94.3 cm	37.25 in 94.6 cm	37.5 in 94.9 cm	37.5 in 95.3 cm	37.75 in 95.6 cm	37.75 in 95.9 cm

PATTERN PIECES

1. **Bodice Front**
   Cut 1 fabric on fold, 1 lining on fold

2. **Bodice Back**
   Cut 2 fabric, 2 lining

3. **Midriff**
   Cut 1 fabric on fold, 1 lining on fold

4. **Skirt Front**
   Cut 1 fabric on fold

5. **Skirt Side Front**
   Cut 2 fabric

6. **Skirt Pocket Bag**
   Cut 2 lining

7. **Skirt Back**
   Cut 2 fabric

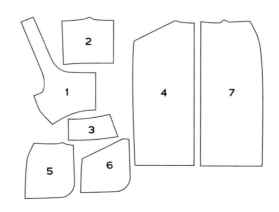

REQUIRED YARDAGE & CUTTING LAYOUTS

Note: All pattern pieces are shown in a "without nap" layout. You may need additional yardage for directional prints, stripes, plaids, and other prints that need to be matched across seamlines.

Fabric (1, 2, 3, 4, 5, 7)

	Sizes 2–10	Sizes 12–20	Sizes 18–34
45 in	3⅛ yds 2.9 m	3⅛ yds 2.9 m	3⅜ yds 3.1 m
60 in	1⅞ yds 1.7 m	2⅝ yds 2.4 m	3⅛ yds 2.9 m

KEY TO LAYOUTS

☐ Right side of pattern piece

▦ Wrong side of pattern piece

Be sure to note whether the pieces are cut on a double or single layer of fabric. For a double layer, there will be a note indicating FOLD on the layout.

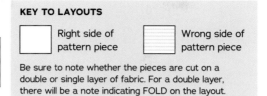

45 in, all sizes

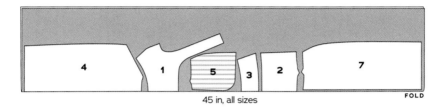

60 in, sizes 2–10

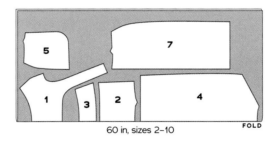

60 in, sizes 12–20

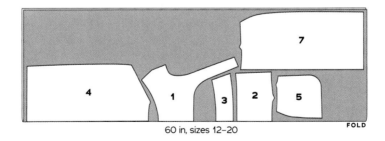

60 in, sizes 18–34

Lining (1, 2, 3, 6)

	Sizes 2–10	Sizes 12–20	Sizes 18–34	Sizes 18–34
45 in	1 yd .9 m	1¼ yds 1.1 m	1⅜ yds 1.3 m	1½ yds 1.4 m
60 in	¾ yds .7 m	¾ yds .7 m	2⅛ yds 2 m	2¼ yds 2.1 m

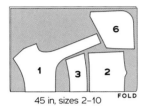

45 in, sizes 2–10

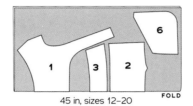

45 in, sizes 12–20

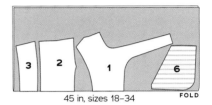

45 in, sizes 18–34

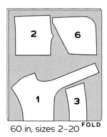

60 in, sizes 2–20

60 in, sizes 18–34

ELASTIC CUTTING CHART

Sizes 2–20	2	4	6	8	10	12	14	16	18	20
Elastic Length	13.25 in 33.7 cm	13.5 in 34.3 cm	13.75 in 34.9 cm	14 in 35.6 cm	14.25 in 36.2 cm	14.5 in 36.8 cm	14.75 in 37.5 cm	15 in 38.1 cm	15.25 in 38.7 cm	15.5 in 39.4 cm

Sizes 18–34	18	20	22	24	26	28	30	32	34
Elastic Length	14.75 in 37.5 cm	15 in 38.1 cm	15.25 in 38.7 cm	15.5 in 39.4 cm	15.75 in 40 cm	16 in 40.6 cm	16.25 in 41.3 cm	16.5 in 41.9 cm	16.75 in 42.5 cm

Lillian Jacket

This shapely jacket is named for Lillian, the wife of Adolph Schuman, founder of the Lilli Ann clothing company. Of course, Lilli Ann was famous for its princess coats (as we delved into in Chapter Three) but equally as celebrated for its hourglass-silhouette suits. The Lillian Jacket takes its inspiration from those curvaceous suits with a flared peplum, structured torso with twelve panels, turned-back cuffs, and tailored *shawl collar*. Pair it with the Camille Sheath (skirt or dress version) for a fully suited-up look that hearkens back to the most elegant of vintage coordinates.

I've spent a lot of time studying Lilli Ann jackets and found they achieved their dramatic shape through wildly flared peplums, of course, but also through the use of many panels. Rather than just the standard eight-panel jacket (with princess seams in the front and back), many Lilli Ann jackets had twelve panels and more. I loved this approach for a new pattern, because more seams mean more shaping opportunities. Inspired by the use of additional panels, I designed the Lillian Jacket to have both armhole and shoulder princess seams, with the *apex* of the bust situated between the two. This also means that the pattern pieces are narrower than usual, which allows for creative cutting layouts, as well as creative color-blocking, like the version on pages 186–187. I also found that many Lilli Ann jackets utilized turned-up, shaped cuffs. I love the structured look they provide (plus another opportunity for contrast fabric). Of course, any *New Look*–era jacket was not complete without a shawl collar and statement buttons.

I'll say it again: I highly recommend that you make a *muslin* of this style! The additional panels allow for more fitting seams, so you can take the seam allowances in and out as needed in key areas. Don't forget to look at the length of the jacket between the bust and waist, ensuring that the narrowest part sits exactly at the smallest part of your torso. This stunning version that Susie is wearing is made in cherry red velveteen to mix and match with her Camille Sheath. What a femme fatale!

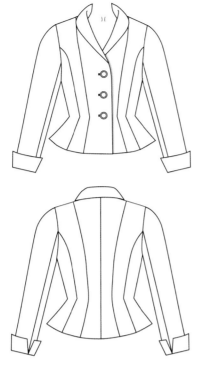

FIT NOTES

The Lillian Jacket is more close-fitting than other jackets, with 2½ to 3 in (6.4 to 7.6 cm) of ease in the bust and ½ in (1.3 cm) of ease in the waist. If you'd like to make a jacket to wear over bulkier layers of clothing, you may wish to size up or add width to the waist.

FABRIC NOTES

We recommend mid-weight wovens: Suitable types include wool crepe, twill, sateen, linen, flannel, lightweight suitings, and tweed.

For the lining, we recommend: charmeuse, crepe de chine, taffeta, and other lining fabrics..

For the underlining, we recommend: muslin.

SUPPLIES

- Fabric for the jacket
- Lining fabric
- Muslin underlining
- 3½-in by 8-in (8.9 by 20.3 cm) rectangle of fabric, organza, and fusible interfacing for bound buttonholes
- Three 1-in (2.5 cm) buttons or covered button kit
- One pair thin to medium shoulder pads
- Thread

INSTRUCTIONS

1 Underline all outer fabric pieces with muslin.

2 Make bound buttonholes on underlined jacket center front. I like to use one rectangular patch to cover all buttonhole marks, and then clash the patch into three separate patches for each buttonhole. (Check out the companion video for a step-by-step tutorial.)

3 Reinforce stitching lines on underlined jacket center front undercollar and cut diagonally to circle. Sew undercollar dart and press toward collar (A).

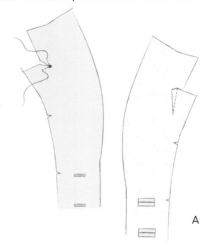

A

4 Staystitch, clip, and notch front princess seam allowances. With right sides together, stitch underlined jacket center front to jacket middle front, and jacket middle front to jacket side front, easing as needed. Press seam allowances open.

5 Stitch fronts RS together at back collar seam. Press seam allowances open. Steam collar into shape, following the roll line (B).

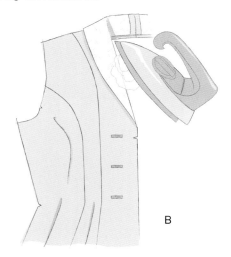

B

6 Stitch jacket center backs together at center back seam. Press seam allowances open.

7 Stitch back princess seams as for front.

8 Staystitch back neckline and clip into curves. Sew jacket front to jacket back at shoulders, right sides together, matching pivot points and center back seams, and pivoting at pivot points. You will need to break your stitching at the dart and restart on the other side of the dart (C). Press seam allowances open and clip away excess at pivot points.

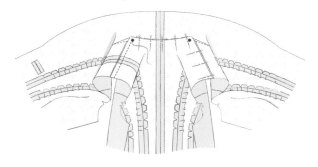

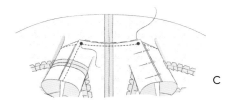

C

9 Sew jacket side seams.

10 With right sides together, sew upper sleeve to under sleeve along inner seam (with single notches). Stitch from armhole to cuff circle, along outer seam (with double notches). Clip seam allowances to cuff circle. Press seam allowances open.

11 Stitch upper sleeve lining to under sleeve lining as in the previous step.

12 With right sides together, sew cuff facing from cuff circle notch to corner to create a ring. Do not stitch the curved edge of the cuff facing. Clip seam allowances to cuff circle. Press seam allowances open.

13 With right sides together, stitch unnotched edge of sleeve cuff facing to sleeve lining hem. Press seam allowances to lining.

14 Pin sleeve lining unit to sleeve, right sides together, along cuff. Stitch, starting and stopping at cuff circle. Grade and notch seam allowances and clip at circles. Turn sleeve right side out. Press flat, rolling seam line toward sleeve. Turn cuff up and steam cuff roll line. On the interior, tack the sleeve facing to the sleeve at the cuff opening seam allowance.

15 Baste sleeve lining to sleeve along upper raw edge, wrong sides together.

16 Gather sleeve cap between front and back notches. Set sleeves into jacket, easing cap as needed. Trim underarm seam allowances and press sleeve cap seam allowances toward sleeve.

17 Tack shoulder pads to shoulder seam allowance by hand.

18 Stitch jacket center back linings together at center back seam. For wearing ease, sew a pleat 1 inch (2.5 cm) away from the center back seam, stitching from the neckline down 2 inches (5 cm) and from the waist notch to the hem. Press pleats to one side (D). Note: be sure you have added the pleat extension to your jacket center back first (see page 191).

19 Turn under lower raw edge of back neck facing and press. Pin wrong side of facing to right side of jacket lining center back and baste along raw edges. Topstitch lower edge of facing to lining.

20 Sew jacket lining front middle/side princess seams, all back princess seams, shoulder seams, and side seams. Press seam allowances open.

21 Sew jacket lining to non-underlined jacket center front along princess seam. Press seam allowances to jacket center front.

22 Staystitch jacket lining around armholes. Clip every ½ inch (1.3 cm).

23 Finish bound buttonhole openings in front facing.

24 Sew lining/facing unit to jacket around neckline and front opening. Clip into seam allowance at the collar roll line. Grade the seam allowances. Understitch the facing.

25 Hand-stitch lining around armholes to enclose seams.

26 Hem jacket with a 1-inch (2.5 cm) hem. Hem jacket lining ½ inch (1.3 cm) shorter than the jacket. Hand-stitch the lining and jacket hem together in between the layers.

27 Hand-stitch bound buttonhole facing to bound buttonhole.

28 Create fabric-covered buttons to match jacket, if desired. Sew on buttons.

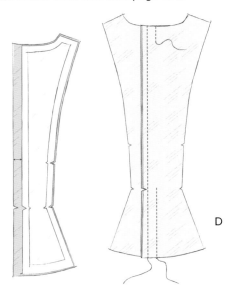

D

HOURGLASS HACK VERSION

Lilli Ann suits often used contrast paneling to create
an hourglass effect, so I was excited to experiment
with this technique. On pieces 3 and 6 (Jacket Side
Front and Jacket Side Back), I created a waistline seam
by drawing a horizontal line from notch to notch (at
the waistline). Next, I cut the pieces along the line and
added a seam allowance to both the upper and lower
half of each piece. Cut the upper pieces (as well as the
front facing) in a darker contrast fabric, and you have a
look worthy of a film noir screen siren.

FINISHED MEASUREMENTS

Sizes 2–20	2	4	6	8	10	12	14	16	18	20
Bust A	33 in 83.8 cm	35 in 88.9 cm	37 in 94 cm	39 in 99.1 cm	41 in 104.1 cm	43 in 109.2 cm	45 in 114.3 cm	47 in 119.4 cm	49 in 124.5 cm	51 in 129.5 cm
Bust B/C	33.5 in 85.1 cm	35.5 in 90.2 cm	37.5 in 95.3 cm	39.5 in 100.3 cm	41.5 in 105.4 cm	43.5 in 110.5 cm	45.5 in 115.6 cm	47.5 in 120.7 cm	49.5 in 125.7 cm	51.5 in 130.8 cm
Bust D/DD	34.5 in 87.6 cm	36.5 in 92.7 cm	38.5 in 97.8 cm	40.5 in 102.9 cm	42.5 in 108 cm	44.5 in 113 cm	46.5 in 118.1 cm	48.5 in 123.2 cm	50.5 in 128.3 cm	52.5 in 133.4 cm
Bust F/G	35.5 in 90.2 cm	37.5 in 95.3 cm	39.5 in 100.3 cm	41.5 in 105.4 cm	43.5 in 110.5 cm	45.5 in 115.6 cm	47.5 in 120.7 cm	49.5 in 125.7 cm	51.5 in 130.8 cm	53.5 in 135.9 cm
Bust H	36.5 in 92.7 cm	38.5 in 97.8 cm	40.5 in 102.9 cm	42.5 in 108 cm	44.5 in 113 cm	46.5 in 118.1 cm	48.5 in 123.2 cm	50.5 in 128.3 cm	52.5 in 133.4 cm	54.5 in 138.4 cm
Waist	24.5 in 62.2 cm	26.5 in 67.3 cm	28.5 in 72.4 cm	30.5 in 77.5 cm	32.5 in 82.6 cm	34.5 in 87.6 cm	36.5 in 92.7 cm	38.5 in 97.8 cm	40.5 in 102.9 cm	42.5 in 108 cm
CB Length, excluding collar	31.75 in 80.6 cm	31.75 in 80.6 cm	31.75 in 80.6 cm	31.75 in 80.6 cm	31.75 in 80.6 cm	31.75 in 80.6 cm	31.75 in 80.6 cm	31.75 in 80.6 cm	31.75 in 80.6 cm	31.75 in 80.6 cm
Bicep	13.5 in 34 cm	13.75 in 34.6 cm	14 in 35.2 cm	14.25 in 35.9 cm	14.5 in 36.5 cm	14.75 in 37.1 cm	15 in 37.8 cm	15.25 in 38.4 cm	15.5 in 39.1 cm	15.75 in 39.7 cm

Sizes 18–34	18	20	22	24	26	28	30	32	34
Bust A/B	45 in 114.3 cm	47 in 119.4 cm	49 in 124.5 cm	51 in 129.5 cm	53 in 134.6 cm	55 in 139.7 cm	57 in 144.8 cm	59 in 149.9 cm	61 in 154.9 cm
Bust C	45.5 in 115.6 cm	47.5 in 120.7 cm	49.5 in 125.7 cm	51.5 in 130.8 cm	53.5 in 135.9 cm	55.5 in 141 cm	57.5 in 146.1 cm	59.5 in 151.1 cm	61.5 in 156.2 cm
Bust D/DD	46.5 in 118.1 cm	48.5 in 123.2 cm	50.5 in 128.3 cm	52.5 in 133.4 cm	54.5 in 138.4 cm	56.5 in 143.5 cm	58.5 in 148.6 cm	60.5 in 153.7 cm	62.5 in 158.8 cm
Bust F/G	47.5 in 120.7 cm	49.5 in 125.7 cm	51.5 in 130.8 cm	53.5 in 135.9 cm	55.5 in 141 cm	57.5 in 146.1 cm	59.5 in 151.1 cm	61.5 in 156.2 cm	63.5 in 161.3 cm
Bust H	48.5 in 123.2 cm	50.5 in 128.3 cm	52.5 in 133.4 cm	54.5 in 138.4 cm	56.5 in 143.5 cm	58.5 in 148.6 cm	60.5 in 153.7 cm	62.5 in 158.8 cm	64.5 in 163.8 cm
Waist	40.5 in 102.9 cm	42.5 in 108 cm	44.5 in 113 cm	46.5 in 118.1 cm	48.5 in 123.2 cm	50.5 in 128.3 cm	52.5 in 133.4 cm	54.5 in 138.4 cm	56.5 in 143.5 cm
CB Length, excluding collar	32.25 in 81.9 cm	32.25 in 81.9 cm	32.25 in 81.9 cm	32.25 in 81.9 cm	32.25 in 81.9 cm	32.25 in 81.9 cm	32.25 in 81.9 cm	32.25 in 81.9 cm	32.25 in 81.9 cm
Bicep	17 in 43.2 cm	17.25 in 43.8 cm	17.5 in 44.5 cm	17.75 in 45.1 cm	18 in 45.7 cm	18.25 in 46.4 cm	18.5 in 47 cm	18.75 in 47.6 cm	19 in 48.3 cm

PATTERN PIECES

1. **Jacket Center Front**
   Cut 4 fabric, 2 underlining

2. **Jacket Middle Front**
   Cut 2 fabric, 2 underlining, 2 lining

3. **Jacket Side Front**
   Cut 2 fabric, 2 underlining, 2 lining

4. **Jacket Center Back**
   Cut 2 fabric, 2 underlining, 2 lining
   (Add 1 inch (2.5 cm) to center back seam
   allowance of lining for wearing ease.)

5. **Jacket Middle Back**
   Cut 2 fabric, 2 underlining, 2 lining

6. **Jacket Side Back**
   Cut 2 fabric, 2 underlining, 2 lining

7. **Back Neck Facing**
   Cut 2 fabric, 2 underlining

8. **Upper Sleeve**
   Cut 2 fabric, 2 underlining, 2 lining
   (Cut sleeve lining at lining cutting line.)

9. **Under Sleeve**
   Cut 2 fabric, 2 underlining, 2 lining
   (Cut sleeve lining at lining cutting line.)

10. **Sleeve Cuff Facing**
    Cut 2 fabric, 2 underlining

11. **3½-in by 8-in (8.9 cm by 20.3 cm)
    Bound Buttonhole Patch**
    Cut 1 fabric, 1 organza, 1 interfacing

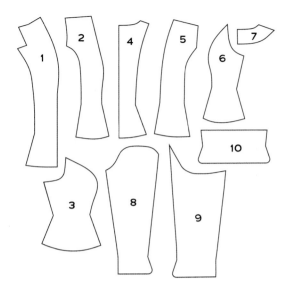

REQUIRED YARDAGE & CUTTING LAYOUTS

Note: All pattern pieces are shown in a "without nap" layout. You may need additional yardage for directional prints, stripes, plaids, and other prints that need to be matched across seamlines.

Fabric

(1, 2, 3, 4, 5, 6, 7, 8, 9, 10)

	Sizes 2–20	Sizes 18–34
45 in	3¼ yds 3 m	3⅜ yds 3.1 m
60 in	2⅜ yds 2.2 m	2⅛ yds 2.6 m

KEY TO LAYOUTS

Right side of pattern piece

Wrong side of pattern piece

Be sure to note whether the pieces are cut on a double or single layer of fabric. For a double layer, there will be a note indicating FOLD on the layout.

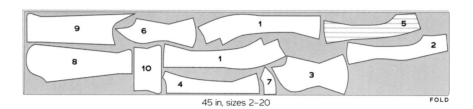

45 in, sizes 2–20

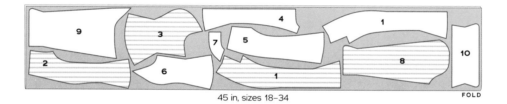

45 in, sizes 18–34

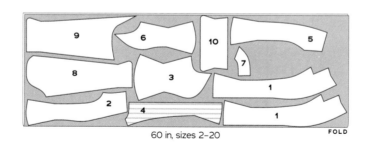

60 in, sizes 2–20

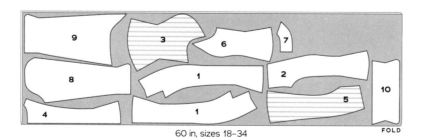

60 in, sizes 18–34

Lining

(2, 3, 4*, 5, 6, 8, 9)

	Sizes 2–20	Sizes 18–34
45 in	2⅛ yds 1.9 m	2½ yds 2.3 m
60 in	1¾ yds 1.6 m	2 yds 1.8 m

Notes:

*Add 1 in (2.5 cm) to center back seam allowance of lining for wearing ease.

For pieces 8 and 9, cut at lining cutting line.

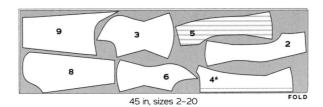

45 in, sizes 2–20

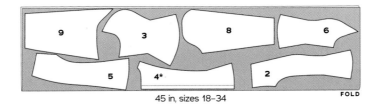

45 in, sizes 18–34

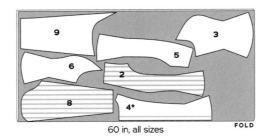

60 in, all sizes

Note: Before cutting your lining, make sure to add a 1-inch (2.5 cm) pleat extension to the center back jacket piece.

Underlining

(1, 2, 3, 4, 5, 6, 7, 8, 9, 10)

	Sizes 2–20	Sizes 18–34
45 in	2⅝ yds 2.4 m	3⅛ yds 2.9 m
60 in	2¼ yds 2.1 m	2⅜ yds 2.2 m

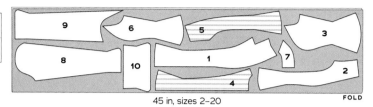

45 in, sizes 2–20

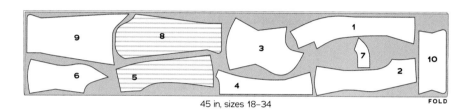

45 in, sizes 18–34

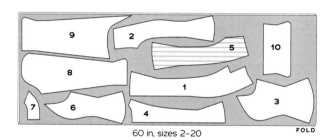

60 in, sizes 2–20

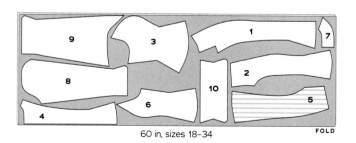

60 in, sizes 18–34

GLOSSARY

APEX   The fullest point of the bust, often (but not always!) corresponding to where your nipple is located. Darts point to the apex, ending 1 to 2 inches (2.5 to 5 cm) away, depending on your cup size. Princess seams usually run across it.

ARMSCYE   A fancy word for armhole. Technically, the armscye is on the bodice and the armhole is on the sleeve.

BASQUE WAISTLINE   A beautiful way to emphasize the waistline. A basque waist bodice is tightly fitted and extends past the waistline over the high hip, coming to a point at the center front. You'll often see it in wedding dresses and other formal gowns.

BIAS   A diagonal grainline on fabric yardage. True bias is the 45-degree diagonal grainline exactly between the crosswise and lengthwise grains. Garments cut on the bias have some natural mechanical stretch and drape beautifully. Bias binding and bias tape are often used to enclose raw edges and curved hems, as they can be easily manipulated around the curve.

BLOCK   When making a garment sloper, the pattern pieces of the sloper become the pattern block. This block is used in flat pattern drafting. At Charm, the block for our 2-to-20 size range is different from the block used for our 18-to-34 size range. We also use different blocks for woven vs. knit designs. If you want to start pattern drafting, creating your woven pattern block is a great place to begin.

BLOUSON   A style of garment where the waistline is fitted but the bodice is full, causing the fabric to blouse out at the waist. It's a comfortable garment that gives you a lot of range of movement. You'll see this style in casual blouses, dresses, and bomber-style jackets.

BODY   Fabric with body has structure and often stiffness. It will stand out from the curves of your body when worn. It's the opposite of drape.

BONING A narrow length of metal, plastic, or other material sewn into the seams or boning casing of a garment to give it support and structure. I prefer using spiral steel boning because it's strong, durable, and flexible. Many fitted dresses of the 1950s will have boning used in the bodice, but you may also find it in swimwear, waistbands, and strapless tops.

BONING CASING or **BONING CHANNELING** A fabric tube sewn (usually) to the inside of a garment's lining or underlining to hold the boning. Boning casing is stronger and more tightly woven than bias tape, so it's a better choice when using boning in a garment.

BOX PLEAT These dramatic pleats are two opposing folds that meet. They are usually somewhat substantial, and can be used in conjunction with knife pleats in a skirt (i.e., you may see a box pleat at center front or center back, with knife pleats on either side). One of my favorite features is to have multiple box pleats on top of each other to provide extra fullness in a '50s style skirt.

BREAK POINT The point where the lapel of a shawl or rolled jacket collar flips from the inside to the outside, located just above the top button.

CORSELET An inner corselet is a foundation garment traditionally made from cotton tulle (also called bobbinet) and spiral steel boning. In couture garments, an inner corselet is integrated into a dress so no other foundation garments need to be worn.

CUT-ON SLEEVES A type of sleeve where there is no seamline between the sleeve and the bodice; they are cut together from one piece of fabric.

DIRNDL This refers to a Bavarian folk costume, but also to a type of skirt common in vintage silhouettes. A dirndl skirt is a simple full skirt that is made with a rectangle of fabric gathered into a fitted bodice or waistband.

DRAPE Fabric with drape has a fluid look and will closely follow the curves of your body when worn. It's the opposite of *body*.

DRAPING A pattern drafting technique, using fabric on a dress form. Unlike flat pattern drafting, which is done with two-dimensional paper, fabric draping allows you to design in three dimensions and is very useful when creating complex designs.

DUPIONI A type of silk fabric with a fine weave that is slubby, opaque, and has a crisp hand. It's a little heavier and thicker than shantung and is a gorgeous fabric to use on special-occasion dresses.

EASE The difference between the measurements of your body and the measurements of your garment. When the garment is bigger, you have positive ease. The more positive ease you have, the looser the garment. When your garment measures smaller than your body, you have negative ease and a tighter garment.

FASHION FABRIC The fabric everyone sees when you do a twirl in your outfit. Fashion fabric can be inexpensive cotton broadcloth or a gorgeous luxury silk, but it's always what people will notice first.

FISHEYE DARTS This is a double-ended dart, seen in a garment without a waist seam. Imagine how a waist dart on a bodice and a skirt dart would meet each other at a waistline seam. A fisheye dart puts those two darts seamlessly together! Note that it is best to sew a fisheye dart from the center to one end, tying your tails off rather than back stitching. Next, flip the work around and repeat for the other end of the dart, overlapping your stitching in the middle of the dart.

FLAT PATTERNMAKING or **FLAT PATTERN DRAFTING** A super-fun process of translating the design you have in your head onto paper pattern pieces. Pattern drafters start with a basic pattern block and then create the style lines and design elements on the two-dimensional paper. The three-dimensional version of this is called pattern draping and happens when you manipulate fabric over a dress form.

GRADING   The PATTERN GRADER uses math (and specialty software) to create additional sizes of a sewing pattern from the base size. You can grade your own patterns when you are between sizes or when your measurements correspond to multiple dress sizes (for example, when you are a size 12 bust and size 10 waist, you will draw a line to grade between the two sizes to create your unique pattern piece).

GROSGRAIN   A type of woven fabric ribbon that has a ribbed texture. It is firm, sturdy, and does not curve or stretch, making it perfect for waist stays. Petersham is similar, but has a scalloped edge that can be curved with steam (as long as it is made from a natural fiber like cotton or rayon).

HAND   How a fabric drapes on your body. Fabric with a stiff and firm hand (called body) will be more structural and stand away from your body. Fabric with a loose and fluid hand (called drape) will skim closely over the curves of your body.

INTERFACING   A specialty fabric designed to give a garment structure and support. Interfacing is often used in cuffs, plackets, collars, facings, waistbands, and anywhere else where you want to increase the body or durability of the fabric. Interfacing can be fused or sewn to your fashion fabric or lining.

KNIFE PLEAT   Sharp pleats, often spaced very closely together, that are all folded in the same direction.

LANTERN SLEEVE   One of my favorite dramatic sleeves! This design is shaped, believe it or not, like a lantern: full in the middle and tapering inward at the top and bottom. It may or may not have gathers. A lantern sleeve is usually achieved by a horizontal seam at the fullest part of the sleeve, but it can also be achieved through strategic gathering and added length to a short sleeve, as in the Bryant Gown (page 89).

MERRY WIDOW   A feat of lingerie engineering! This strapless longline bra was made to cinch the waist, support the bust, and anchor your stockings, all in one. The fifties' answer to the corset, the merry widow was made with a combination of stretch and non-stretch fabrics and heavily structured with steel boning. Designed with a three-part bra cup for extra perkiness and ending at the upper hip, it was the perfect thing to wear under strapless and strappy dresses. The merry widow got its name from the 1952 film *The Merry Widow* with Lana Turner, when Warner's created a bra inspired by the film. You can now buy reproduction merry widows from companies like the UK-based What Katie Did.

MIDRIFF   Often seen with shelf bust designs or other bodices where the bust is emphasized, a midriff is the section of the bodice between the underbust and the waist. If there is a front midriff pattern piece, there is sometimes a back midriff piece as well.

MITERED   An easy way of finishing a corner without adding extra bulk. Instead of folding the raw edges on top of each other, they are sewn at a 45-degree angle, with the excess trimmed away.

MUSLIN or TOILE   A test garment sewn to perfect the fit of a pattern before cutting out more expensive fashion fabric. Muslins are often made with cheap cotton muslin (calico) fabric. When making a muslin, you only need to sew the bodice and fitted parts of the garment, without the lining or facings. Creating a well-fitting muslin is key to a making a well-fitting finished garment, so don't skip this step!

NEGATIVE EASE   Ease measures the difference between your body and your garment. With negative ease, the garment is smaller than your body's measurements. Negative ease is very common in stretch knit garments and cinching shapewear pieces, designed for a tightly fitted garment.

NEW LOOK   A hugely popular style of women's clothing in the early 1950s that emphasizes hourglass curves with rounded shoulders, a prominent bust, nipped-in waist, and padded hips. The style was created by Christian Dior in 1947 and is the classic silhouette of the fifties.

PAD STITCHING   A hand-sewing technique often used in tailoring to attach two or more layers of fabric together. Pad stitching adds body, structure, and support, and can create a nicely rolled collar or lapel. To pad stitch, take small stitches along the length of the fabric, spacing the stitches closely together.

PIVOT (WHEN STITCHING)   A technique for creating a nice, crisp point when sewing a corner. To pivot, stitch your sew line until you reach just before the pivot point, then slow your stitching and use the handwheel of your machine to stop exactly at the point, with your needle down in the fabric. Lift the presser foot, adjust the fabric so it is now positioned in the new stitching direction, lower the presser foot, and start stitching again as normal.

POSITIVE EASE   Ease measures the difference between your body and your garment. When your body measurements are smaller than the garment measurements, you have positive ease. As the ease increases, the garment becomes less fitted.

PRINCESS SEAM   An alternative to darts, princess seams are bodice seamlines that run over the fullest point of the bust, originating at either the shoulder or the armhole. (Imagine if you had a dart at both the shoulder and the waistline of a fitted bodice, and those darts were connected to form a seamline.) Though most fifties garments favored darts for shaping, the princess seam gained more popularity by the end of the decade. It is an elegant shaping solution, and if you have trouble fitting darts on your body, you may wish to give princess seams a go! Though we usually think of princess seams on a bodice, the adjoining vertical seams on a skirt are also referred to as princess seams.

RAGLAN SLEEVE   A garment with a raglan sleeve will have an angled seamline that runs from the front neckline to the back neckline, passing underneath the arm. This style was very popular in the 1950s and was used in dresses, bodices, jackets, and coats.

ROLL LINE   A line that naturally forms when a collar or lapel is worn. It's often helpful to steam the roll line into place during construction so it will hold its shape.

SELVAGE or SELVEDGE   The edge of fabric that has been finished to prevent fraying or unraveling. When a length of fabric yardage is woven or knit on a loom, the selvage runs parallel to the grainline.

SET-IN SLEEVES   One of the most common types of sleeves for garments, this is characterized by a seamline at the shoulder which runs around and underneath the arm, closely fitted to the bodice armscye. The sleeve cap will be eased to the curve of the shoulder and the grainline of the sleeve will be parallel to the floor.

SHAWL COLLAR   A type of collar that rolls directly from the front neckline and shoulder to the lapel, without a separate pattern piece. Shawl collars can be small or dramatic, and are often used on vintage jackets, coats, and dresses.

SHELF BUST   Used commonly to describe any fifties dress that accentuates the bust through ruffles, structural support, ruching, petals, or shirring. The midriff of a shelf bust garment will be closely fitted, appearing to support the drama of the bust decoration.

SHIRRING   A sewing technique that gathers fabric with many layers of parallel stitches. This adds textural decoration but is especially fun and useful when elastic thread is used in the bobbin, creating a panel of fabric with negative ease.

SILK ORGANZA   A gorgeous thin and sheer silk fabric with a plain weave and very crisp hand. I love using silk organza to underline garments for body and structure, as it's so lightweight. It's also lovely as a fashion fabric, when you are looking for something sheer and structured. And it makes a wonderful press cloth to protect your fabric from heat damage.

SLASHING AND SPREADING   A technique for lengthening a pattern piece. To slash and spread, cut the pattern piece perpendicular to the garment's centerline, spread it the desired amount, and then tape a piece of paper into the gap. True the edges at the cut lines.

SLOPER   A garment that is fitted very closely to your body, with minimal wearing ease. A basic sleeveless bodice sloper will have a bust dart, waist dart, and high jewel neckline. You can also create slopers for skirts, pants, and sleeves. The pattern pieces of a sloper are used when flat pattern drafting.

STAND or COLLAR STAND   A small but supportive piece of fabric in between the collar and the bodice, helping the collar to stand up and away from the body. The collar stand is often interfaced and lined, making it even more supportive.

SURPLICE   A bodice neckline that is created when fabric crosses from the shoulders to the opposite waistline, often used in wrap garments. This creates the appearance of a V-neck and of cinching the waistline.

TAILOR'S HAM   A firmly packed pressing pillow about the size and shape of a big hunk of ham. It's invaluable when pressing curved seams.

UNDERLINING   A simple but effective technique used to create body, add structure, or provide coverage. When I'm sewing a lace garment, I'll often underline the bodice with a contrast color of opaque silk to really highlight the lace decoration. To underline your fashion fabric, cut an identical pattern piece from your underlining fabric and sew together within the seam allowances.

UNDERSTITCH   An essential step that helps to roll a facing or lining to the inside of the garment so that it remains hidden. It's often used around a neckline, sleeveless armhole opening, or sleeve hem. To understitch, work from the right side of the garment and stitch about $1/8$ inch from the seamline, being sure that the facing or lining seam allowances are underneath your stitching.

WAIST STAY or WAIST TAPE   A secret length of grosgrain ribbon or twill tape hidden on the inside of your dress at the waistline. It supports the weight of the skirt and helps to relieve tension on a cinched-waist dress. It also makes it a little easier to zip up the dress, if you don't have a helper!

ACKNOWLEDGMENTS

I truly could not have written this book without the support of many, many people and four-legged friends.

First, I have to thank the entire team at Charm Patterns. This book project was truly a Charm production in every way. You allowed me to take the time I needed away from the studio to write and edit the book and design the patterns, while keeping all our many other projects afloat—not a small feat in itself. Most significantly, you were the driving force behind bringing this book project to life, and without you none of this would have been possible.

Andrea Lenci-Cerchiera, production manager, truly made the amazing patterns in this book happen. She managed each of the designs in this book, tirelessly testing and retesting each one until it was perfectly to Charm standards in our full size range. She managed the photo and video shoots, and is my second set of eyes on every project.

Amber Wyatt, patternmaker and grader, created the patterns from my sketches, worked with the team to perfect the fit and style, and graded each one into our full range.

Lindsie Bergevin and George Gott designed the pattern sheets, cutting layouts, and technical charts. Special thanks to Lindsie for creating the first sample layout of the book, which inspired me to keep going with it and helped it find its home at Abrams.

Amy Pascale, administrative assistant, was instrumental in managing the many, many images needed for this book.

Angie Green, managing editor, helped me shape the proposal, provided expert writing assistance on the instructions and more, and kept Charm running the entire time.

Kristen Contrera, associate production manager, helped create samples for the book while managing many other projects.

Mich Conway, sample maker, helped with the sewing for the shoot.

A big thank-you to everyone involved with the photography and video for this book. Shameless Photo has been my longtime creative partner; Angela Altus took the gorgeous pattern photos, while Sophie Spinelle flawlessly edited them. Thank you to my dear friend and gorgeous babe Susie Dahl for modeling. Stevie Rosalie and Missy Firestone both created epic vintage hairstyles you see in photos throughout the book. Meredith Heuer took the studio shots, capturing many moments of real-life beauty amid the chaos.

Thank you to Courey Ayres for several of the photos in the book, and for being a constant friend in so many different ways throughout the years.

As always, thanks to my mom, Patty Sauer, for her encouragement and support.

All my love and gratitude and snuggles to the pets of Charm. Hattie for the endless entertainment in the studio and at home, and Elvira for being the best studio panther we could ask for. Eli and Alfie kept me sane and laughing and cuddling at home. In special memory of my beloved Henry, who was part of the sewing community his whole life and was an angel on earth.

Finally, thank you so much to Shawna Mullen and the entire team at Abrams for being my publishing home for my entire career and continuing to believe in me and my work. Here's to the next one!

PHOTOGRAPHY AND IMAGE CREDITS

All garment and Charm Patterns photographs are by Shameless Photo (Angela Altus), and all behind-the-scenes studio photographs are by Meredith Heuer. All other photos and images as credited below:

Pages 6, 16, 25, 31 (left), 31 (left), 36, 40, 46 (top right), 52, 58 (right), 59, 60 (right), 61 (left), 62, 72–73, 75, 77–78, 80 (right), 82, 84, 86, 91 (left), 92, 94, 102 (top center, top right, bottom left), 103 (bottom), 110, 116, 118–120, 121 (right), 122, 127, 130 (bottom), 131, 132 (right), 136–137, 140 (bottom), 141–144, 157, 160–163, 166, 169–170, 172–175, 179-180, 183, 186-187, 193 by Shameless Photo

Pages 18, 19 (lower left, right), 24 (left), 26–27 by Camille Shaheen-Tunberg

Page 19 (top left) by Villa Rosemaine

Page 31 by Cheshire Vintage

Pages 32 (right), 41 (top left, top right), 44, 45 (top), 58 (left), 80 (left), 89, 90, 97 (left), 98 (right), 100, 105, 114–115 from Alamy

Pages 41 (lower right), 66 (top right, top left), 67, 90 (left), 98 (left), 102 (top left, bottom right), 103 (top), 104, 111 (left), 125 from the Collection of Gretchen Hirsch

Pages 35, 45 (bottom), 48 (bottom), 49, 57 (right), 61 (right), 76, 87, 91 (left), 117, 121 (center), 130 (top), 132 (left), 140 (top) by Gretchen Hirsch

Pages 64, 66 (bottom) © The Metropolitan Museum of Art. Image source: Art Resource, NY

Pages 70, 112 by Red Goose Studios

Pages 96, 97 (center) by Lucy La Riot

Pages 106–109 from L. Tom Perry Special Collections Harold B. Lee Library Brigham Young University

Page 121 (left) from CEEB Swimwear

All illustrations are by Robin Blair except:

Pages 35, 48 (bottom), 76, 87, 117, 140 by Gretchen Hirsch

ABOUT THE AUTHOR

Gretchen "Gertie" Hirsch got her start as a blogger with the popular *Gertie's New Blog for Better Sewing*, and has collaborated with Butterick and Simplicity on the "Patterns by Gertie" line of sewing patterns and designed fabrics for Joann Fabrics, Spotlight Stores, and Michael Miller. A sought-after instructor, Gertie has traveled the world to lead sewing workshops highlighting her techniques.

In 2017, Gertie launched her own independent sewing pattern line called Charm Patterns, focusing on new women's clothing designs inspired by classic looks from the forties and fifties. In 2020, she launched her Patreon subscription service, which includes monthly downloadable patterns and accompanying video tutorials, virtual sewing circles, live streams, and more. It has amassed a large community of passionate sewing enthusiasts from around the world.

She is the author of five other books published by Abrams, including *Gertie Sews Jiffy Dresses*, *Gertie's Ultimate Dress Book* and *Gertie's New Book for Better Sewing*. She lives in Newburgh, New York.

Editor: Shawna Mullen
Designer: Anna Christian
Design Manager: Darilyn Carnes
Managing Editor: Lisa Silverman
Production Manager: Kathleen Gaffney

Library of Congress Control Number: 2023946470

ISBN: 978-1-4197-6956-6
eISBN: 979-8-88707-095-7

Text copyright © 2024 Gretchen Hirsch
Photography and image credits can be found on page 204

Cover © 2024 Abrams

Printed and bound in China

10 9 8 7 6 5 4 3 2 1

Abrams books are available at special discounts when purchased in quantity for
premiums and promotions as well as fundraising or educational use. Special editions
can also be created to specification. For details, contact specialsales@abramsbooks.
com or the address below.

Abrams® is a registered trademark of Harry N. Abrams, Inc.

ABRAMS The Art of Books
195 Broadway, New York, NY 10007
abramsbooks.com